PEYTON MANNING

PRIMED

AND

READY

BY

JIMMY

HYAMS

ADDAX
PUBLISHING
GROUP

Published by Addax Publishing Group Inc.
Copyright © 1998 by Jimmy Hyams
Designed by Randy Breeden
Cover Design by Jerry Hirt

For Information address:
Addax Publishing Group
8643 Hauser Drive, Suite 235, Lenexa, KS 66215

ISBN: 1-886110-58-61-1

Distributed to the trade by Andrews McMeel Publishing
4520 Main Street
Kansas City, MO 64111

1 3 5 7 9 10 8 6 4 2

Printed by T.V. Allen USA
Library of Congress Cataloging-in-Publication Data

Hyams, Jimmy, 1955-
    Peyton Manning : primed and ready / by Jimmy Hyams.
        p. cm.
    ISBN 1-886110-61-1
    1. Manning, Peyton. 2. Football players—United
States—Biography. 3. Tennessee Volunteers (Football
team) I. Title.
GV939.M289H93 1998
796.332'092-dc21
    [B]
                                                            98-35609
                                                            CIP

Dedication

To Melanie, Leslie and Valerie, who wondered why I spent so much time working when I was supposed to be on vacation. And to my ill Mother. She's always been my inspiration.

"I had a feeling if I went to Ole Miss, I'd be an instant celebrity without doing anything,"
> - *Peyton Manning on picking UT and not Ole Miss, where his dad was an All-American quarterback. Jan. 26, 1994.*

"If Peyton and his daddy were the same age, his daddy would have to watch him play. ... He's the best high school quarterback I've ever seen,"
> - *Ole Miss coach Billy Brewer on Peyton Manning, February 1994, which violated NCAA rules that prohibit coaches from talking about prospects.*

"No, coach, he (Peyton) can't come to the phone right now. He's outside smoking a cigarette,"
> - *One of Manning's high school friends playing a practical joke by answering the phone and pretending he was talking to a recruiter. (Manning does not smoke). Feb. 3, 1994.*

"I don't think Danny Wuerffel can hold a candle to him. Peyton's even a better quarterback than that guy (Drew Bledsoe) the New England Patriots have,"
> - *Former Heisman Trophy winner Earl Campbell, Aug. 14, 1996.*

"I've done crazier things than stay four years at Tennessee, like coming to Tennessee in the first place (instead of Ole Miss),"
> - *Manning said. August 1996.*

"One more year, one more year,"
> - Chant of UT fans during the final minutes of UT's win over Northwestern in the Citrus Bowl. Olivia Manning later said she thought the chant was a factor in her son's decision to return to UT. Jan. 1, 1997.

"I made up my mind, and I don't expect to ever look back. I am going to stay at the University of Tennessee,"
> - Manning said at a press conference announcing his decision. March 5, 1997.

"He promised me books, tuition, food. I get to call one play a game, and I get to drive his Lexus around the block every now and then,"
> - Manning on what Fulmer promised him if he'd stay at UT another year. March 5, 1997.

"Peyton Manning. Gator Bait again,"
> - Headline on Sports Illustrated cover the week after Florida beat the Vols for the fifth straight year. Sept. 16, 1997.

"I feel sorry for Peyton. He came back to play another year against Florida. I'm sorry we didn't protect him better,"
> - Guard Spencer Riley after Manning was knocked down 11 times and sacked twice in Florida's 33-20 win. Sept. 20, 1997.

Table of Contents

Acknowledgments

THIS WAS MY FIRST BOOK. IT WASN'T EASY. CHANGING jobs at midstream didn't help. I went from assistant sports editor at *The Knoxville News-Sentinel* to a sports talk-show co-host at Knoxville radio station WNOX. However, I had people to interview, research to complete, pictures to take, negatives to develop, and text to write. How does John Grisham do it?

First, I must thank my wife Melanie, for her patience and assistance. She even forgave me when I forgot our eighth wedding anniversary the week of my deadline. OK, honey, if the book sells, you'll get a new kitchen.

Thanks to my in-laws, Lib and Boyd Sharpe. I set up camp at their house so I could write this book.

Thanks to the fine folks at Newman High School for assisting me during my trip to New Orleans: Lori Ochsner and coaches Tony Reginelli, Frank Gendusa, Butch Farris and Jeff Brock.

Thanks to Harry Moskos, Mike Keith, John Adams, Bob Hodge, Steve Ahillen, Brent Hubbs, Bob Kesling, Barry Rice, Craig Kelly, Todd Stewart, Bud Ford and Cinetel Productions for helping in various ways.

Thanks to all the people who graciously granted me interviews.

Thanks to *The Knoxville News-Sentinel* for supplying photos.

Thanks to Dick Broadcasting Company, for delaying the first day at my new job so I could complete this book.

Thanks to Addax Publishing Group for taking a chance on a first-time author.

And thanks to the Manning family.

Introduction

IN MARCH OF 1995, I WAS TALKING WITH THE COLLEGE football editor of *Lindy's* magazine, Don Borst. He wanted to know about an up-and-coming young quarterback named Peyton Manning.

"He can't miss," I said. "He'll be one of the top five quarterbacks in the nation as a sophomore."

Borst went a step farther. He selected Manning as Lindy's preseason first-team All-American. I couldn't argue. Manning hadn't proven himself as a big-time quarterback yet, but I knew he would. His work ethic, his desire, his competitive nature, his intelligence, all told me he was going to be a great quarterback. He could not miss.

He won't miss in the NFL, either. Yes, pro football is a huge adjustment from college football. But is it any more challenging than going from a Class AA private high school in New Orleans to starting quarterback for a top 10 program in the football-rich Southeastern Conference?

Manning surely will experience a few bumps along the way, but he's got a chance to make Colts' fans forget about what might have been with John Elway. Many NFL experts believe Manning will make the Colts an instant playoff contender.

My wife suggested in the fall of 1997 that I should write a book on Peyton Manning. Not only is his an intriguing story, but Manning is a wonderful person, a great role model, and, simply, the most popular athlete in the history of Tennessee athletics.

His kindness is infectious. When my daughter Leslie, was 4 years old, she already had a crush on Peyton. She was crushed when Tennessee was upset by Memphis in 1996. I paint myself as an objective observer of the teams and players I cover. My family is another matter. Leslie had seen how forlorn Peyton looked during television interviews following the Memphis defeat. She wanted to write Peyton a letter. I took dictation. It started something like this:

"Dear Peyton:

"You look better with your helmet on."

I'm sure she scored points with that one. Nonetheless, the letter was delivered and Peyton responded, without being asked, by autographing a picture for Leslie.

I guess I should have known someday I would write a book about my daughter's favorite player.

Peyton's favorite player was his father. Archie Manning was a legendary quarterback in the Southeastern Conference. Archie's humble demeanor, personality and sage advice made it easier for Peyton to be his own man and to succeed beneath his father's shadow.

From the get-go, Peyton Manning wanted to be a quarterback, just like his dad. From his workout sessions to his film-study, Peyton had a purpose. He would prove room existed for two great quarterbacks in the same family.

"I look back on it now, watching the old tapes of him, and I see it better," Archie Manning said. "Everything about him says it. He was supposed to be a quarterback."

Peyton became Tennessee's first All-American quarterback since 1930. He was a Heisman Trophy runner-up. He set 33 Tennessee records, seven SEC records and two NCAA records. He evolved into one of college football's all-time great quarterbacks.

Manning's brilliant college career, sense of civic duty and genuine kindness elevated him to legendary status in Tennessee, the same honor afforded his father in Mississippi. Make no mistake, Peyton Manning is a folk hero in Tennessee.

Peyton Manning accomplished one feat in college his father didn't. Peyton won an SEC Championship. Now, he'd like to one-up his father another time. Archie never played in an NFL playoff game. Peyton would love nothing better than to lead the Colts into the playoffs.

As a high school prospect, Peyton Manning carried a "can't miss" label into college. He brings the same label to the Indianapolis Colts. Here's the story of why Peyton Manning is primed and ready for the NFL.

Peyton Manning wanted to wear the same number in college his dad wore at Ole Miss (18). But 18 belonged to Tennessee defensive back DeRon Jenkins. Nos. 12 and 16 were available. Peyton took 16 at the suggestion of older brother Cooper, who said 12 was a number for backup quarterbacks.

Like Father, Like Son

"It's been neat to have your hero in
your own living room"
— *Peyton Manning*

PEYTON MANNING GRABBED THE AUDIO TAPE, SLIPPED
it into the tape player, parked himself in bed and listened intently.

He visualized the field at Vaught-Hemingway Stadium in Oxford, Miss.
He saw the colors of the Ole Miss Rebels and LSU. He saw the colors
of Ole Miss and Alabama, of Ole Miss and Southern Miss, of Ole Miss
and Mississippi State. He imagined the Rebels driving from left to right,
or right to left.

He heard the booming voice of Stan Torgenson announce the players'
names, and young Peyton Manning memorized that lineup. He
remembers they all were from Mississippi, and he can still recite some of
it.

"The Rebels have the ball to start.

"Mitchell from Biloxi

"Coleman from Clarksdale

"Winter from Biloxi

"Jernigan from Jackson

"McClure from Hattiesburg

"Poole the tight end from Oxford

"Franks split wide to the right

"Myers to the left."

Then Peyton would add his own flare.

"The 6-3 red-head from Drew, Manning, brings them to the line. He drops back, scrambles, throws a long pass. Touchdown! Touchdown Ole Miss!"

Older brother Cooper Manning was into Archie's pro career. Not Peyton. He loved college football. And he loved listening to radio cassettes of his father's college games.

"It was just fun for me to do," Peyton said. "That's when I started to love the SEC and realized it was a special conference."

He also realized he was the son of a special player, a special person. Archie Manning was Peyton Manning's hero.

"He was my favorite player growing up," Peyton said. "That's why I wanted to know everything about him, in his college era and pro era. Then, as I got older, he was still my hero. Not just because of the football player he was, but the person he was.

"It's been neat to have your hero in your own living room."

Peyton Manning's winning attitude got an early start around the Manning home. Baseball and basketball were extracurricular activities for Peyton. Football was his passion. He grew up around it. He went to see Saints games when his father was the quarterback. He went with his mother and older brother. In 1980, when the Saints were in the midst of a 1-15 season, Archie Manning was awful during a 27-7 loss to the Los Angeles Rams. He had 96 passing yards and two interceptions.

Fans booed.

"Can we boo, too?" four-year-old Peyton asked his mother. Before waiting for an answer, Peyton and six-year-old Cooper started booing.

"We thought it was fun to boo," Cooper said. "We didn't know what booing meant. We weren't booing our dad."

Didn't matter.

"After that," Olivia said, "I left the kids home for a while."

But staying home didn't stop them from getting into playful mischief. A

Chapter 1 – Like Father, Like Son

New Orleans tour bus taking in the Garden District would routinely make a stop in front of the Mannings' house. Cooper and Peyton would go outside to the front yard, throw passes to entertain the on-lookers, then Peyton would fake a leg injury and hobble inside. The tourists were left stunned.

Peyton wasn't afraid to speak his mind at an early age. When he was 9 and Cooper 11, Olivia informed the boys that Archie, now playing for the Minnesota Vikings, decided to play one more season.

The year before, the Mannings made Minneapolis their fall and winter home. This time, there was a vote.

"We can either move up north for the season again or stay here," Olivia said. "Now, your daddy loves us very much, but ..."

Peyton interrupted: "It's too cold up there."

Olivia: "You're right, dear. It certainly is. "Archie braved the Minnesota cold alone for one more year before retiring after 14 seasons in the NFL.

The Manning kids entered the world more like lineman than skill-position players. Cooper weighed 12 pounds 3 ounces. Peyton weighed 12 pounds 1 once. Eli weighed 9 pounds 14 ounces. "We thought something might be wrong with Eli," Olivia said. Each of the kids grew to be at least 6 feet 3 inches tall. Each was a multisport athlete.

"I don't think the athletic ability of the three could be differentiated," said M.K. Phillips, who coached all three Mannings in summer league baseball. "The mindset could be. Peyton, without a doubt, is the most intense athlete I've ever been around. He always wanted to be successful, and he knew what it took."

He had a good teacher. As a youngster, Peyton the quarterback would walk up behind the center a bit bowlegged like Archie. The catch was, Peyton's legs were straight. Friends would laugh. Peyton wanted so much to be like his dad. It was comical to the family.

"It's almost aggravating sometimes," Cooper said. "Dad won't be in the room, but there is Peyton, talking in the same lingo and giving orders just like if dad was doing it. He's a carbon copy of dad." Not in appearance, but in the way he thinks and acts.

Like father, like son.

Peyton's freshman year at Tennessee, he often responded to a question by saying, "As my dad would say ..."

Archie told Peyton one summer evening in 1995, "When you go back to school this year, and you talk to the media, please stop saying, 'As my dad would say...' I'm not your coach. I just want to be your father."

The next night, Peyton was sitting in his father's car, doing a call-in radio show. Archie was in another vehicle. A few minutes into the show, Peyton started an answer: "Like my dad says ..."

Archie laughed: "I can't believe it."

Archie should believe it. Peyton is an independent thinker. He's not a clone. But he's smart enough to realize Archie Manning is not a bad role model to emulate as a player and as a person.

Some athletes complain of undue pressure or expectations because they have a famous father. Not Peyton.

"I resent it when I hear sons of famous athletes use those excuses," Peyton says. "I love my father and I admire him. I try to be like him.

"At an early age, I tried to accept it. In every article that's written about me, it's going to say, 'Peyton Manning, son of former Ole Miss and Saints quarterback. ... I'm certainly proud that I'm Archie Manning's son.

"I never treated it as a burden."

A burden? It was a blast. Peyton went to games with his hero, played games with his hero. His hero watched HIM play games. If Peyton had a question, his hero was always there to answer. They did typical father-son stuff together.

Sure, sometimes Peyton would have liked to escape the public eye. But rather than detach himself from his father, he wanted to be just like Archie.

Peyton wanted to wear the same football numbers as his father. He would be No. 14 in high school, No. 18 in college and No. 8 in the pros. That changed, however. He switched from 14 to 18 as a high school junior after he learned his older brother, Cooper, who wore No. 18 at Newman High School, had to quit the sport because of spinal stenosis. Peyton wore No. 18 in honor of Cooper.

"When you grow up in New Orleans in the Manning house, football is important to you," Peyton said. "For doctors to say, 'Cooper, your career is over,' it was tough for him. I thought that's the least I could do, changing to his number."

Cooper loved football, but not like Peyton.

"It was tough on Cooper (to give up football)," Archie said, "but no doubt, it would have been tougher on Peyton."

Peyton agrees.

"I'm the kind of guy who, during football season, might be doing a paper, then all of the sudden, put my pen down, sit back and think about the game for about 30 minutes," Peyton said. "If I had to go through a fall without football, I don't know how I'd handle that."

In college, Manning wanted to wear No. 18 but cornerback DeRon Jenkins had that number. "I wasn't going to be a guy who said, 'I'm not going there because I want 18,'" Manning said.

Manning didn't want a single digit. Nos. 12 and 16 were his only available choices. Peyton asked Cooper, the family's number expert, for advice.

"You can't wear No. 12 in college; that's a backup's number," Cooper said.

Manning picked 16.

"Swamp Rat," said Archie, referring to the nickname of Dewey Warren, a former star quarterback at Tennessee in the mid-1960s.

Peyton didn't make wearing a jersey number an issue, just as his father didn't in 1971 when he was the first-round pick of the New Orleans Saints. When Archie was drafted, his picture was splashed across the front page of the *New Orleans Times-Picayune* with Saints jersey No. 18. But that number belonged to a defensive back, Hugo Hollis. Not one to upstage a veteran, Archie settled for No. 8.

Like father, like son.

Archie Manning was known as much for his running ability as his passing accuracy during an All-American career at Ole Miss. Though never as fast as his father, Peyton wanted to be an option quarterback in the seventh grade.

When Peyton was a freshman in 1994, he threw a fourth-down pass to a covered receiver against Alabama on a last-minute drive. On the opposite side of the field, a running back was wide open.

Tennessee coach Phillip Fulmer said Manning threw to the wrong side. Manning challenged his coach, saying he threw to the side he was coached to throw to. Manning was right.

Archie Manning also had a fiercely independent streak. In 1974, the NFL players were on strike. Archie Manning joined four teammates on the picket line at the rookie camp in Vero Beach, Fla. Saints owner John Mecom Jr., attacked Manning.

"We've had a difficult time developing a leader on the field, and that includes Mr. Manning," Mecom said. "I've been very disappointed in some of his actions the last couple of weeks. I hope he tries as hard on the field to be a leader as he is off the field."

Archie Manning may be polite, but he's also prideful.

"If he wants to get into a debate on leaders, I don't see what ground he's got to walk on," said Archie, then a three-year NFL veteran. "He (Mecom) has been the leader seven years now. If I'm to blame for the past three years, who's to blame for the other four?"

It was an unusual public war-of-words for Archie Manning.

"It's not my way to get into controversial situations," Archie Manning said. "That's not the way to run a successful franchise. But I'm not going to sit here and take it."

Archie stood up to authority, just like Peyton did after that Alabama game in 1994.

Like father, like son.

In 1970, Ole Miss coach John Vaught called Archie Manning, "The greatest college quarterback I have ever seen." But football wasn't Archie's only sport. He was an outstanding shortstop on the Ole Miss baseball team.

Out of high school, Archie was drafted by the Atlanta Braves. Out of college, he was drafted by the Kansas City Royals. Why pick pro football over pro baseball?

"My wife doesn't like baseball," Archie said.

Peyton was a fine baseball player in his own right. Some thought he had major college potential as a third baseman. But his position was shortstop. Why? Because that's the position Archie played.

"Peyton wanted to play shortstop, like his father," said Billy Fitzgerald, Peyton's baseball coach at Newman High School.

Like father, like son.

Archie Manning broke his left arm during his senior season in 1970 and spent days in a Memphis hospital.

Peyton Manning suffered an infection from a ruptured bursa sac in his right knee during his senior season and spent days in a Knoxville hospital.

Both injured as seniors. Both spent days in a Tennessee hospital.

When Archie was in high school, he broke both legs and his left arm. His only full season of play was his senior year. After he broke his arm as a junior, his father asked: "Son, is it worth it?"

Archie: "Yes, dad, this and more."

Peyton worked diligently to return from that ruptured bursa sac to play in the Orange Bowl. Because it was worth it.

Like father, like son.

Archie's phone bills to Knoxville were outrageous Peyton's first two years at Tennessee. Father and son talked at least twice a week. They talked about school, academics, football.

"His father is his main support," said former Tennessee offensive lineman Will Newman, Manning's roommate when both were freshmen. "He'd call his dad all the time during the season and ask for advice. Sometimes, you could hear his dad's voice rise on the other end: 'Quit being so hard on yourself, Peyton.'"

Like Archie, Peyton doesn't refuse signing autographs. After a Tennessee practice, as he walked off the field, he'd sign hats, programs, paper, T-shirts. Tennessee finally instituted a "no-autograph policy after practice" to protect Manning from the barrage.

After the 1995 Alabama game, a woman asked Manning to sign the blue jeans she was wearing on her rear. "I was afraid to say no," Manning said. "I didn't want her to think I was a jerk." So, with the boyfriend as a witness, Manning signed the woman's blue jeans.

Before Manning's junior season, he had signed about 15,000 autographs. In December of 1995 alone, he signed at least 5,000 autographs. Ellie Wilson, a former Tennessee football secretary who was eventually given a special job to help handle Manning's schedule, had a stack of paraphernalia three feet high near her desk in September 1996, all seeking Manning's autograph.

"Peyton was getting 25 Sports Illustrated's a day," Wilson said of the issue that featured Manning on the cover. "It's been pouring in like a fire hydrant broke and here comes the water." Requests came from Seattle, California, Boston, New Orleans, Washington D.C.

As a freshman and sophomore, Peyton set aside 30 minutes a week to sign autographs. But as the demands increased, he was overwhelmed.

"Sometimes I'd walk by Ellie's desk, see the stack and just walk away," Manning said.

But eventually, he would get to most of them. And eventually, Tennessee imposed a policy forbidding Manning from signing helmets, jerseys, hats or footballs - anything but flat objects — for fear those items could be resold at sports shops or at auctions. Manning also started personalizing his autographs by writing, for example: "To: Billy Brewer, Peyton Manning."

Some autograph hounds tried to use their influence. "We'd get letters from Mississippi fans saying, 'I'm your 14th cousin, 12 times removed,' " Wilson said.

Wilson estimates Manning signed about 250,000 autographs while at Tennessee.

Archie faced unusual autograph demands in college, as well. After Ole Miss lost 33-32 to Alabama on national television in 1969, a game in which Archie set an SEC record with 540 total yards, Archie got 5,000 pieces of mail the next week.

"At that point coach Vaught got one of the secretaries to be in charge of my mail," Archie said.

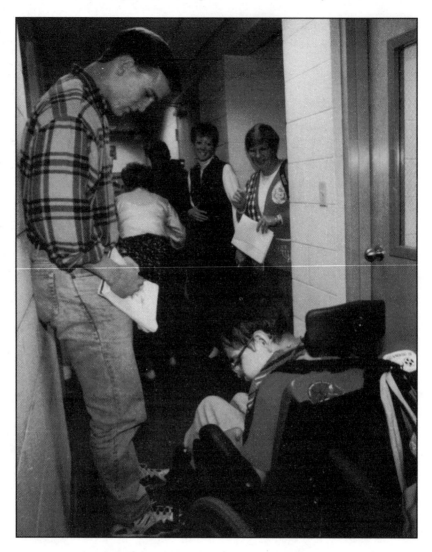

During one of his numerous public appearances, Peyton signed an autograph for a handicapped youth. Manning signed an estimated 250,000 autographs during his four-year Tennessee career.

Like father, like son.

Archie was so popular in college, he had a song written about him, "The Ballad of Archie Who?"

The title was inspired, in part, by a former Tennessee linebacker, Steve Kiner. Responding to a question about Manning in 1969, Kiner said:

Chapter 1 – Like Father, Like Son

"Archie Who?"

The song was written by the Rebel Rousers and was played to the tune of Johnny Cash's "Folsom Prison Blues":

"The ball is on the 50, the down is third-and-10;

"He runs it down the sideline, yes Archie takes it in.

"He plays for the Ole Miss Rebels, Archie Manning is his name;

"The best dad-burn quarterback who ever played the game.

"The ball is snapped to Archie, the down it is the last;

"He throws it to the end zone, another touchdown pass.

"He puts points on the scoreboard for that big Rebel crew;

"That's All-American Archie, you know, Archie who?

"Now here in Mississippi, he's not a one-man team;

"We've got lots of Rebels who really are on the beam.

"But I bet they all will tell you, that old Archie is the boss;

"Just ask ole hee-haw Kiner if he's not a real stud hoss.

"They try to make the tackle; they wonder where he went.

"Archie super Manning should run for president.

"He wears that No. 18 for the big, bad red and blue;

"The rootin' tootin' quarterback, my friend, that's Archie who

"A rootin' tootin quarterback ....."

The song sold 50,000 copies.

Archie's days with the Saints weren't as much fun as his college experience. Despite being a two-time pro bowl quarterback and a most valuable player of the National Football League, Manning never played on a winning team in New Orleans. He never played on a playoff team.

"He was a great quarterback playing with crappy teams, but he never came out in the newspaper or TV and knocked a teammate," Peyton

Archie Manning is gang tackled by his two sons, four-year-old Cooper (top) and two-year-old Peyton, shortly after Archie was selected the 1978 NFC Player of the Year. The sons used to take turns giving their daddy a back rub after games.

said. "That's what I remember more about him than his athletic ability. He just got trapped with a bad, bad, bad, franchise."

After Tennessee lost to Florida in 1997, a battered and beat up Peyton Manning apologized to Vol fans, took blame for the loss and said of his offensive line, which played a terrible game: "They did the best they could; that's all you can ask."

Like father, like son.

Peyton's memories of his father's NFL career aren't positive.

"I remember him coming home, and obviously they had lost many of those games, but you couldn't tell, because he was kind of the same," Peyton said. "He was very level headed. He was real sore, but he took time for us."

Archie used to challenge Cooper and Peyton to see who could give the best back rub.

"All right, Cooper, your turn," Archie would say.

Ten minutes later, Archie would say: "Peyton, you get a shot."

The winner?

"It's kind of close," Archie would say. "Better keep going."

Peyton: "By that time, all the soreness was out of his body. He used to trick us. But it taught me a lot. You might as well stay the same, win or lose."

Dr. Larry Fields has been the pastor at Central Baptist Church in Knoxville since 1986. As a young minister in Summitt, Miss., in 1969, he was invited to a Rotary Club meeting in McComb, Miss., about two miles from Summitt. The guest speakers: Ole Miss football players Floyd Franks and Archie Manning.

Manning already was a hero figure in Mississippi. One of Fields' deacons asked Fields to get two Manning autographs - one for the deacon's daughter and one for the deacon.

Fields remembers Archie having a good sense of humor and a gift for speaking. "He could laugh at himself," Fields said.

Twenty-five years later, Fields, who became the Tennessee football team chaplain in 1993, is listening to another Manning speak. He has a sense of humor. He has good communication skills. It's like seeing a young Archie Manning.

Like father, like son.

"I never dreamed I'd connect with Archie again when his son was a college student," Fields said.

Fields counts among his blessings the relationship he has developed with the Manning family. "It's been a privilege for me to deal with Peyton Manning and the Manning family," Fields said.

Fields said Peyton was a more polished speaker than Archie when they were the same age. "Peyton had a more stable family situation than his dad did," Fields said. "One of the reasons I admire Archie so much is he maintained his faith and stability after the tragic (suicide) death of his father (1969)."

Peyton had almost 100 percent attendance at Tennessee's voluntary pre-game chapel services, even if it meant hopping on a freight elevator at a motel and taking a back door or two to avoid a throng of well-wishers and fans seeking his autograph.

"Peyton always felt that was an important part of his pre-game preparations," Fields said. "He could have easily used the excuse, 'If I go down for chapel, I'll get inundated,' but he wanted to come."

When Peyton was a sophomore, Archie was the guest speaker at a chapel service. Two years later, Peyton gave a testimony to the team along with kicker Jeff Hall.

Like father, like son.

While at Tennessee, Peyton Manning spoke to churches, schools, the 4-H Club. He was chairman of a read-a-thon. He went to the Greater Knoxville Boys and Girls Club. He put in hundreds of hours of community service.

Peyton did what he had seen his father do in New Orleans.

"I see so much of Archie in Peyton and Peyton in Archie," said Tennessee trainer Mike Rollo, whose role provides him with a unique perspective of Peyton and the Mannings.

"Peyton didn't have to sign everything, all those dang footballs. It would get to the point where you'd get sick of the stuff. Teammates asked him to sign things. And he'd always do it.

"Peyton always aimed to please. Peyton wants to fit in. Peyton wants to help out."

Like father, like son.

Newman football coaches Tony Reginelli and Frank Gendusa, said they had no qualms about coaching the son of arguably the greatest quarterback in SEC history. Why? Because they knew Archie was a class act and wouldn't interfere.

"I wasn't going to be one of those Little League fathers," said Archie. For that, Peyton was appreciative.

Tennessee offensive coordinator David Cutcliffe was asked if he had reservations about coaching the son of a great quarterback.

"I'll say this, I thought about that briefly," Cutcliffe said. "I have a whole lot of confidence in what I do. I'd like to have coached Archie," he says with a smile. "I'd like to coach Joe Montana's son when he's old enough. I'd loved to have coached Joe Montana."

Manning's closest relationship in Knoxville was with Cutcliffe. Asked if Peyton was like a son to him, Cutcliffe said: "I don't know that I thought he needed a father. He's a really good friend. He's the type person you like being around, period. My mood changes when I see him."

Then, Cutcliffe reconsidered.

"Yes, he was like a son. I could be in the worst of moods and be having a miserable day. Then I'd see him and immediately change from that perspective, like you do when you see your kids.

"I can still see him coming down the hall with that big old notebook, energized and ready to go. He's a guy I can't ever remember getting on my nerves. I enjoyed the chance to coach a guy like that."

The comparisons between Peyton the quarterback and Archie the quarterback were inevitable. Peyton was the better drop-back passer, Archie the better runner. Peyton was a better student of the game, in part because he had to be. Football defenses weren't as complex when

Archie played, especially in college.

Their arm strengths were similar, their field awareness acute.

Peyton's passing statistics are far superior to his father's in terms of yards, touchdowns, touchdowns-to-interception ratio and completion percentage. But Archie was good enough to be voted the SEC quarterback of the half-century (1933-82). He was the SEC quarterback of the decade in the 1960s and 1970s, even though he played just one year in the '70s.

"I shouldn't say this, but I think Peyton wants to be better than his dad," said Newman's Fitzgerald. "Not so he can brag; it's just a goal to push him."

A modest father tips his hat to his son: "He's better than I was."

Peyton Manning played before the largest crowd to ever watch a college game, 107,608. He played before almost a million fans a year during his four-year Tennessee career. Millions more watched him on television.

But one man never saw Peyton play. Never will.

Elisha Archibald (Buddy) Manning Jr., died of a self-inflicted gunshot wound in 1969, after Archie Manning's sophomore season at Ole Miss. The reason: bad health caused by a stroke.

"Since I got in college, I've thought about that more," Peyton Manning said in December 1997.

Does Archie regret that his father didn't get a chance to see Peyton play?

"Sure," Archie said. "I regret he didn't get to see me play but one year in college."

Peyton and Archie rarely talk about Buddy Manning. A couple of summers ago, Peyton said he asked his dad's mother, Sis Manning, and his maternal grandparents, Cooper and Frances Williams, more about what Archie was like in college, what he was like after games.

"I feel like his father could have told me the most," Peyton said. "It bothers me a lot he couldn't see my dad play. He saw him as a sophomore, but he never knew what my dad did at Ole Miss."

Archie was always by Peyton's side to help his son make tough decisions. Archie wasn't so fortunate growing up. His father took his life after Archie's sophomore season at Ole Miss.

Peyton noticed that when Cooper became a sophomore at Ole Miss, then later when Peyton became a sophomore at Tennessee, Archie got closer to his sons.

"My dad wanted to tighten the screws as far as our relationship," Peyton said. "I sensed that about my father, just always wanting to be there for me. I'm sure a lot of that has to do with his relationship with his father. He didn't have one after .... "

Buddy Manning was manager of a farm machinery company in Drew, Miss. Business wasn't good at times because he had trouble collecting bills.

"Mississippi Delta farmers were like that," Archie said. "They'd harvest their crop and spend money on new cars and vacations before they paid for any farm equipment."

But that's not what got to Buddy Manning.

"It was health," Archie said. "He'd had a stroke. He was real stubborn. He didn't like doctors and hospitals. It was just a low point."

Archie found his father dead in their home.

"It was tough," Archie said. "But I was glad I did rather than my mother or sister (Pam)."

Archie cleaned things up before they got home.

"More than anything, I think what I regret was he didn't get to see me play when I got into pro ball," Archie said. "Maybe if I went to a golf tournament somewhere, I could have taken him with me. Or I could have introduced him to some players. Or done some neat things with him. I regretted that somewhat.

"Peyton doesn't know much about my dad. He was older before I told him how my dad took his life. It's hard to explain to someone who didn't know him."

Eva Pack knew Buddy Manning. Eva grew up in and around Drew. Buddy once sponsored Eva in a Drew High School organization. She's about eight years older than Archie.

"Buddy was the nicest guy and had the cutest personality," Eva Pack said.

News of Buddy's suicide rocked Drew and Mississippi because, by then, Archie already had attained celebrity status.

Two years after Buddy died, Eva Pack's father also died, taking his life like Buddy did. Eva's father, a farmer, was an alcoholic. One of the first people to offer condolences was Sis Manning.

"It must have been painful for her to do that," Eva Pack said. "My family will never forget her support at that time. You see, caring about others is characteristic of this fine family."

Sis Manning never saw Peyton play in person, either. She once lost some luggage on an airplane trip going to watch Archie play in a Saints game and had to call her daughter for help. She decided if she had to depend on others while traveling, she wouldn't go to any more games.

Her worst college experience, ironically, occurred in Knoxville. In 1968,

Archie threw six interceptions in an embarrassing 31-0 defeat at Tennessee.

"She said it was the longest day of her life," Eva Pack said. "The Ole Miss people were getting on Archie. She said she didn't feel like she had a friend in the world."

Years ago, Sis Manning gave Archie a poem. It was written by General Douglas MacArthur. It's called, "A Father's Prayer."

Archie uses it to close some of his speeches.

"Build me a son, O Lord, who will be strong enough to know when he is weak, and brave enough to face himself when he is afraid; one who will be proud and unbending in honest defeat, and humble and gentle in victory.

"Build me a son whose wishbone will not be where his backbone should be; a son who will know Thee - and that to know himself is the foundation stone of knowledge.

"Lead him, I pray, not in the path of ease and comfort, but under the stress and spur of difficulties and challenge. Here let him learn to stand up in the storm; here let him learn compassion for those who fall.

"Build me a son whose heart will be clear, whose goal will be high; a son who will master himself before he seeks to master other men; one who will learn to laugh, yet never forget how to weep; one who will reach into the future, yet never forget the past.

"And after all these things are his, add, I pray, enough of a sense of humor, so that he may always be serious, yet never take himself too seriously. Give him humility so that he may always remember the simplicity of true greatness, the open mind of true wisdom, the meekness of true strength.

"Then I, his father, will dare to whisper, 'I have not lived in vain.'"

Archie Manning has not lived in vain.

During the recruiting countdown, Manning went against the grain and signed with Tennessee rather than follow his dad's footsteps and go to Ole Miss. Peyton didn't want to play in the shadow of his father, where Peyton would have been hailed as a savior of a struggling program.

Chapter Two:

Saying No to Ole Miss

"Being Archie Manning's son, no matter where I go, it'll be pressure"
– Peyton Manning

IT'S 1993, THE FIRST DAY COLLEGE COACHES CAN CALL prospects at home. Peyton Manning invites more than a dozen friends to his house.

Manning's buddies take turns answering the phone.

Tom Osborne. Lou Holtz. Bobby Bowden.

With each ring, a different person answers, wondering which coach is calling next.

The phone rings again.

"Hello," says one of Peyton's friends.

"No coach, he's not here. He's outside smoking a cigarette."

Peyton Manning freaks out. He invited friends over to have a good time, but this was going too far. He races over to grab the phone.

"Peyton's a tight kind of guy," said friend Nate Hibbs. "He wants everything to go smooth."

This wasn't going smoothly. On the other end was coach .... well, it wasn't a coach. It was a schoolmate. Thad Teaford had walked upstairs into the bedroom of Peyton's younger brother Eli and dialed the family's phone number, pretending to be a coach.

Peyton Manning had been had.

The recruiting process was fun for Manning - at first. He enjoyed the attention. He enjoyed visiting with big-time college coaches. He enjoyed recruiting trips.

He had an alphabetical file on each team that piqued his interest. He could tell you each quarterback on the roster, each receiver, what kind of offensive line they had, the classification of each player.

"I'm enjoying it a hundred percent," Manning said in December 1993. "From Day One, my dad and I decided it would be a fun process. I can't see how anybody wouldn't enjoy it. But my mom is getting burdened a little bit."

Manning narrowed his list to six schools: One Big Ten school, Michigan; tradition-rich Notre Dame; perennial powers and passing teams Florida and Florida State made the cut. Ole Miss, where Peyton's father was an All-American, was in the hunt. So was Tennessee, though many considered the Vols a long shot.

Would Peyton be subjected to more pressure if he followed in his father's footsteps and played for Ole Miss?

"The way I see it," Peyton said, "being Archie Manning's son, no matter where I go, it'll be pressure. Being the son of a former quarterback, they expect you to do well. Going to Ole Miss will be more pressure because that's where my dad made his name."

Peyton had a plan. He would make his five official visits and take an unofficial trip to the school with which he was most familiar, Ole Miss. He would announce his decision at a Jan. 25, 1994 press conference.

As time drew near, the recruiting process began to overwhelm Manning. Would he get away from the South and play at Michigan? For a while, Archie thought that's where his son would go. Would the Golden Dome and mystique of Notre Dame lure him? Florida State was a football power with a throwing reputation. But the Seminoles weren't in the SEC. And when it came down to it, Peyton was an SEC man.

That left three schools. Florida was hot under Steve Spurrier. Tennessee was a bitter rival of Ole Miss during his father's playing days. And how could he say no to Ole Miss? His father is the only football player in Rebels' history to have his number retired. His mother was homecoming queen at Ole Miss. His brother, who signed to play football at Ole Miss, was still attending the school.

Chapter 2 – Saying No to Ole Miss

It had to be Ole Miss, didn't it? Archie wouldn't let him go anywhere else, would he?

That's what Ole Miss fans thought. That's what Ole Miss fans hoped.

The telephone rang at the house of Isidore Newman High School head football coach Tony Reginelli. It was 6:30 a.m. on Jan. 25. The caller was Peyton Manning. He'd been hiding out in a motel for a couple of days, trying to sort through this thing. He had reached a decision.

"Coach," Manning said, "it comes up orange. It's Tennessee."

One by one, Manning called his high school coaches to deliver the news. One by one, he called the college coaches.

It was Tennessee.

Tennessee! Are you kidding?

It was a shock to me, really," Reginelli said. "I thought it'd be Ole Miss."

Frank Gendusa, Manning's offensive coordinator at Newman, thought Manning was going to Florida.

Mike Keith, a former Knoxville sports talk-show host and a Tennessee football historian, said Manning's decision to attend Tennessee was akin to Gen. Dwight Eisenhower's son becoming a general in the Russian army.

Nobody at Newman thought it was Tennessee. Nobody. But everybody at Newman knew one thing: All hell was about to break loose in Mississippi. And it did.

After Peyton Manning made his decision known to the coaches, he held a press conference that afternoon at the Hilton in downtown New Orleans. The media turnout was huge. Two months shy of his 18th birthday, he faced the press like a schooled politician. He explained why he picked Tennessee. He said five schools - Ole Miss, Florida, Florida State, Michigan and Notre Dame - finished second.

"I felt like I was saying no to so many more people than just (Ole Miss head coach) Billy Brewer," Peyton said. "I felt like I was saying no to all my relatives who had gone to school there, and a lot of friends who were there."

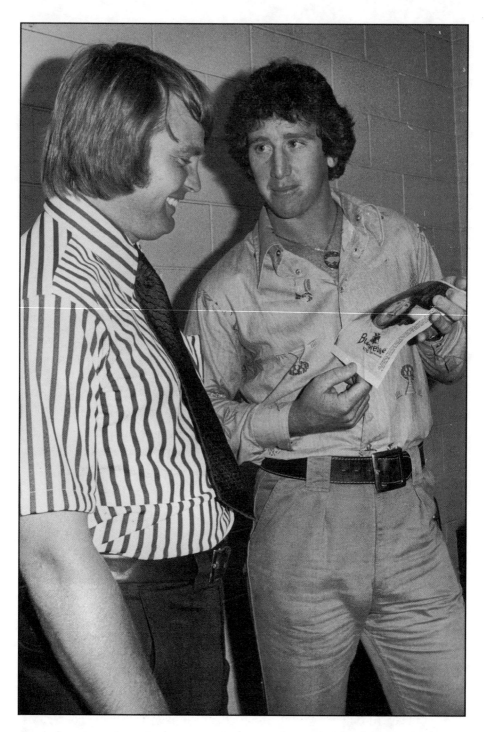

Archie Manning (right) elicits a laugh from his backup quarterback with the New Orleans Saints, Bobby Scott. Ironically, Manning's son, Peyton, and Scott's son, Benson, became teammates at Tennessee. Bobby Scott, a former Tennessee quarterback, was one of the few who predicted Peyton would sign with Tennessee.

Said Reginelli: "That was the toughest press conference I've ever been to in my life. To me, it took a lot of fortitude to go to Tennessee. But as classy as Peyton is, he handled it with ease and the utmost professionalism."

Archie Manning looked like a whipped puppy. On what should have been a joyous occasion for the Mannings, some Ole Miss fans were going to make sure Archie and his family paid for their displeasure. Archie knew it was coming.

"Archie and Olivia looked like they were going to a funeral," said Bo Ball, a close friend of Archie's. "They were under so much pressure."

"Archie was drained," said Reginelli, who sat next to Olivia Manning at the press conference. "It was hard for him. It was probably one of the hardest times of his life. You felt for him, knowing his loyalty to Ole Miss."

The son of Ole Miss' favorite son was going elsewhere. Ole Miss fans felt betrayed. They called Peyton a traitor. Archie got hate mail, nasty threats. *The Jackson* (Miss.) *Clarion Ledger* installed a special line to field calls the day Manning announced he would attend Tennessee. More than 2,500 people called by 9 a.m. The total reached 5,270 by late afternoon. Hundreds of other calls flooded the sports department.

"Somebody needs to get a whip to that boy," said one disgruntled Rebel fan.

Four-letter words of disgust flew off tongues.

"I believe that one day in the distant future, after Peyton has finally matured, he will look up the word `loyalty' in the dictionary and realize that, for selfish reasons, he let down many people who considered him part of the Ole Miss family," Paul French of Jackson, Miss., wrote in a letter to the *Clarion-Ledger*. "People (in Mississippi) are ticked off," said *Clarion-Ledger* sportswriter Mike Knobler.

Newman High got 86 letters the day after Peyton's announcement, 60 the next. Reginelli read them all.

"Some had tire tracks on them," Reginelli said. "Some had `Archie Who?' buttons that were smashed. Some had state lines that said, `Don't cross.'"

If only they had known what Reginelli knew: "Archie recruited for Ole Miss until the end. He always said that. He'll tell you that."

One month before Peyton's announcement, Archie said: "I feel strongly about the fact it should be Peyton's decision. If he wants to play football there (Ole Miss), that's fine. If it's not the best thing for him, that's fine. I love Ole Miss but I can't say I love Ole Miss more than my son. I love him more.

"I guess it goes without saying, Ole Miss probably wouldn't be in Peyton's mix if not for the relationship with me and his brother there."

Newman got its share of letters supporting Manning. Reginelli showed those to Peyton. "I didn't think he needed to see the bad ones," Reginelli said.

The Mannings were cursed by none other than Butch Veazey, an All-SEC tight end at Ole Miss in the early 1970s and a long-time acquaintance of Archie's. Three years later, Veazey's son Burney, would commit to Ole Miss, renege, then sign with Tennessee.

Peyton knew his decision would disturb Ole Miss fans. He knew his father would catch unmerciful grief. Yet, he rejected Ole Miss anyway. What does that say about Peyton? Better still, what does it say about Archie?

"Archie made Peyton feel that it was not a factor in him making his decision," Gendusa said. "What Archie was saying was, `What I'm interested in, as a parent, is your happiness; do what you want to do, and I'm man enough to deal with whatever comes my way.'"

It came, buddy. It came.

Ole Miss had wanted to unretire Archie's No. 18 and give it to Peyton. Archie had six season tickets to Ole Miss games and gave a hefty annual donation to the athletic department. A recruiting room is named after Archie. Archie was national chairman for an Ole Miss fund-raising drive that raised about $8 million for athletics.

Archie was Ole Miss.

But Archie's son said no to Ole Miss.

"It hurt me," Ball said. "I just couldn't imagine Peyton going anywhere but Ole Miss. It almost felt like a loss in my family."

Ole Miss is smaller than most SEC schools. That intimacy helps enhance the bond between school, student and alumni. Ole Miss is family to a lot of folks. And the Mannings were practically the first family of Ole Miss.

Archie was the All-American quarterback who revived memories of Ole Miss glory days. From 1952-63, Ole Miss lost more than two games in a season only once. The Rebels won four SEC championships, produced two unbeaten teams and were voted the SEC's team of the decade for the 1950s.

Ole Miss' glory days ended in 1964 when the Rebels went 5-5-1. Four years later, Archie Manning took over. During Manning's three seasons at quarterback (1968-70), Ole Miss was capable of beating any team in the country. In 1969, Ole Miss handed Tennessee and LSU their only regular-season losses, then upset third-ranked Arkansas in the Sugar Bowl.

"Archie came along and became a folk hero," Ball said. "Archie Manning was like a god at Ole Miss."

Ole Miss was in worse shape in 1993 than it was when Manning revived the program some 25 years earlier. In 1993, the Rebels were 6-5 and on the brink of NCAA probation. They needed a savior. They needed Peyton Manning.

"They were counting on Peyton taking us to the top of the mountain," Ball said.

That was a concern to Peyton, who would say after signing with Tennessee: "I would have been an instant celebrity (at Ole Miss). But I was 18 years old, not a savior."

Ole Miss fans vented their frustration at Archie Manning.

"Archie got a lot more ugly letters than you realize," Ball said. "He won't admit it, but it hurt him. I can tell you that. Some people just never did understand."

During one trip to Oxford, some angry Ole Miss fans at a gas station advised Archie to stay out of the state. He would soon learn he wasn't wanted for as many instate speaking engagements as usual. Olivia became worried about her husband's trips to Mississippi. "He has his head on a swivel now and that is a shame," she said in the summer of 1995.

Three years after Peyton's decision, most of the bitter feelings subsided. Peyton went to an Ole Miss game and was treated like a celebrity, signing autographs. Archie has a good relationship with new Ole Miss coach Tommy Tuberville.

But not everyone has forgotten or forgiven.

"Some guy writes two or three times a year," Archie said. "He says, 'I hope he (Peyton) breaks his leg.' I don't think he's an Ole Miss graduate because he doesn't spell very well."

Several things contributed to Manning's decision to select Tennessee. Sources said Archie privately questioned the way Ole Miss coach Billy Brewer ran his program. Also, the Mannings knew Ole Miss was about to get hit with NCAA sanctions and probation for recruiting violations. "Peyton said, 'Will I be able to compete (for an SEC championship)? Will I be on television? Will I get the exposure?'" Reginelli said.

Moreover, Tennessee and Michigan did the best job of recruiting Manning, and in the end, Manning wanted to play in the SEC.

Tennessee also afforded Manning an opportunity to play the quickest. The Vols had a senior quarterback in Jerry Colquitt and no apparent successor. Manning would be on equal footing competing for the starting job in 1995. Florida had Danny Wuerffel, who had set a national freshman record for touchdown passes in a season. Florida State had a hotshot redshirt freshman, Thad Busby.

Finally, and most importantly, Manning's older brother, Cooper, had been diagnosed with narrowing of the spinal canal in the fall of 1992, ending his career. Cooper signed with Ole Miss in February 1992. Had Cooper been playing at Ole Miss, Peyton says he "probably" would have signed with the Rebels.

There's no "probably" about it, said people close to the Manning family. Had Cooper been playing at Ole Miss, Peyton Manning would have become a Rebel with a cause.

"Peyton always wanted to play with his brother," said Newman assistant coach Bradley "Butch" Farris, an Ole Miss graduate whose father, cousins and uncles attended Ole Miss. "Peyton said at one time, if Cooper hadn't had his neck problem, he would have gone to Ole Miss."

Dr. Landrump Leavell II, then an interim pastor at First Baptist Church of New Orleans, the Manning's church, recalled a similar conversation with Peyton Manning in January 1994.

"Peyton told me, 'If Cooper was still playing football at Ole Miss, there's no question where I'd go,'" Leavell said. "He'd talked to Cooper and Cooper had cleared it if he decided on Tennessee."

Cooper's misfortune was Tennessee's fortune. But the Vols didn't luck into Peyton Manning. They did a marvelous recruiting job, starting with recruiting coordinator and running backs coach Randy Sanders, who works most of Louisiana for the Vols.

Sanders laid the groundwork, then head coach Phillip Fulmer made a home visit, then offensive coordinator and quarterbacks coach David Cutcliffe helped close the deal.

Cutcliffe and Manning hit if off immediately. Almost before Cutcliffe found a seat in the Manning house on 1420 First Street in the plush Garden District of New Orleans, Peyton was filling the room with questions. What is your approach to teaching and coaching the quarterback progression? How do you plan to develop a quarterback's technique? Will I redshirt? If someone gets hurt, what are your plans for me now and in the near future? How many quarterbacks will you sign?

"The first day I talked to Peyton, I knew he was an unusual guy," Cutcliffe said. "He had done a lot of work in preparing for the recruiting process. He seemed open (to Tennessee), but like everybody else, you thought, 'How could he not go to Ole Miss?' His dad wasn't just a player at Ole Miss. He was the best player in the history of Ole Miss' football program. There's a difference in saying your dad just played at Ole Miss."

Given that hurdle going in, Cutcliffe gave it his best shot. He'd been recruiting in plenty of living rooms. But this Manning kid wasn't like anyone else he'd encountered. Peyton's questions were pointed and meaningful. They had content and depth.

Cutcliffe realized then that Peyton Manning was in control of his recruitment, that he was the decision maker - not his father, not his mother, not his brother or some uncle.

"He was the best listener I'd ever talked to as a 17-year-old," said Cutcliffe. "He was a great question-asker. When I walked away, I felt like he and I had connected in our first face-to-face visit. I felt really good. When I got on the plane and flew out of there, I felt energized."

Tennessee was recruiting four quarterbacks that year: Manning, Branndon Stewart of Texas, Ryan Clement of Colorado and John David Phillips of Alabama. There was a fifth quarterback the Vols did not recruit. It was a wise decision.

The fifth quarterback was Josh Booty of Shreveport, La. Booty had better statistics in high school than Manning, and many rated Booty a better prospect. An undercurrent of competition developed between the Mannings and the Bootys. Tennessee knew it couldn't get both quarterbacks. Booty was interested in LSU, the home-state university, and he was a great baseball prospect who would be drafted high by a major league team. You could win the battle by signing Booty, then lose the war by his going to pro baseball.

Tennessee went after Manning.

"I liked Peyton Manning better than Booty," Cutcliffe said. "I thought Josh Booty was a thrower and Peyton Manning was a passer. I thought Booty was just slinging the ball in the shotgun. I thought Peyton had rhythm and timing and better accuracy."

LSU signed Booty, and Booty signed a $1.6 million contract with the Florida Marlins.

Cutcliffe didn't think Manning was as impressive on high school film as Heath Shuler of Bryson City, N.C., who signed with Tennessee, or Tim Couch of Hayden, Ky., who signed with Kentucky. "But after getting to know Peyton, he was the best total package," Cutcliffe said.

Meanwhile, Fulmer was feeling uncomfortable at the Manning house. While Cutcliffe and Peyton were foaming about football, Fulmer was looking for a bullet-proof vest.

Olivia Manning, the mother with a keen memory, asked Fulmer two questions: "Does Steve Kiner still come around Tennessee?" and "Do you play Ole Miss in the next four or five years?"

Tennessee coach Phillip Fulmer didn't have much to smile about after making his home visit to recruit Peyton Manning. Olivia Manning asked two questions that put Fulmer on the spot. But Fulmer was all smiles after Manning started wearing orange.

"Oh, great, mom," Peyton said.

In 1969, Steve Kiner was an All-American linebacker for Tennessee. During preseason interviews, a sportswriter asked Kiner if he thought Ole Miss could contend for the SEC championship. Kiner compared the Rebels to mules. When asked about Archie Manning, Kiner said: "Archie who?" Kiner claims he was misquoted, but his teammates - Fulmer included - didn't offer much support for that contention.

In 1969, Ole Miss beat Tennessee 38-0 in what became known as the Jackson (Miss.) Massacre.

As to Olivia's second question, well, Fulmer fibbed.

"No, they're not on our schedule," Fulmer said.

In truth, Tennessee would play Ole Miss in 1996 and 1997.

"He lied," Peyton said, laughing. "I forgive him for that. But I could tell he felt this is a long shot because of what my mom was asking."

To Fulmer's credit, he didn't interrupt when he saw the bond growing between Cutcliffe and Manning. A more egotistical head coach would have. Instead, Fulmer let Cutcliffe ride the wave.

Peyton didn't care what had happened between Tennessee and Ole Miss, and Kiner and Archie some 25 year earlier. He was interested in the here and now. And he waded into Cutcliffe with a bevy of questions.

"Recruiting is not a time to be bashful. It's a time to ask questions," Peyton said. "I wasn't interviewing them, but I was asking a lot of questions."

Cutcliffe disagrees. He was being interviewed. By a 17-year-old kid.

While Peyton Manning was asking Tennessee questions, one question was being asked at Newman High School: Where is Ole Miss? Why isn't Brewer doing a better job of recruiting Manning?

"I'm going to be honest," said Newman coach Frank Gendusa, "I don't think Ole Miss did a good job recruiting him. I don't know if it was because Coach Brewer thought Manning was in hand. They weren't around here as much as some other schools."

Chapter 2 – Saying No to Ole Miss

Brewer defends his recruitment of Peyton.

"How do you recruit Peyton to Ole Miss when he's been around it, when his room is red and blue, his house is red and blue, he watches film of his daddy playing for Ole Miss?" Brewer said.

Brewer assigned his best recruiter, Keith Daniels, to Peyton. They devised a two-year plan of sending mail and making phone calls. Brewer didn't want to bore Manning — "You can run out of things to say"— so Ole Miss was not a constant presence on Newman's campus.

"We were blamed for that - 'Y'all didn't recruit him hard' - but we were doing it in a different manner," Brewer said.

Brewer scoffs at speculation that he and Archie didn't get along. "That's a bunch of crap," said the retired Brewer, when contacted in May of 1998 at his home in Oxford, Miss. "We never had a cross word. Never."

Brewer said that Cooper and/or Peyton attended almost every football camp he had at Louisiana Tech, then Ole Miss. Archie spoke at Louisiana Tech's sports banquet. Archie helped Brewer start a quarterbacks' camp at Ole Miss. Brewer and Archie both played at Ole Miss, graduating some 10 years apart. Both were on the Ole Miss team of the century.

Brewer watched Archie Manning's son play against Northeast of Zachary in the Class AA state playoffs.

"Peyton was more than I expected," Brewer said. "He was a senior in high school, but he was a sophomore in college mentally. He had a grasp of the game and what was going on out there. He would ad lib and do things that were just unbelievable."

Brewer stood near the Newman bench during the game. At one point, a Newman coach stepped back and tripped over — guess who? — Billy Brewer.

"When Peyton came to the sideline," said Brewer, "I got in the huddle with them. I wanted to make sure he saw me there."

Brewer came away thinking: "He's the best high school quarterback I've seen."

A few days later, Brewer got into trouble bragging about Peyton. It's against NCAA rules for a college coach to talk publicly about a prospect. But Brewer, saying he thought he was off-the-record, told sportswriter Ron Higgins of the Memphis *Commercial Appeal*: "Peyton is as good as I've seen. At this stage, he is way ahead of Archie. He doesn't run as well at this particular time, but the football sense on the field and knowing what to do, how to do it and when to do it, I don't think you can compare them."

That landed Brewer a slap on the wrist from the NCAA. But it had no impact on recruiting Manning, Brewer said. In addition to Cooper's career-ending condition, Brewer blamed Ole Miss' antiquated facilities.

"We were in the Dark Ages, I mean, really in the Dark Ages," Brewer said. "People don't know how bad it was."

Yet another factor, said Brewer, was lack of administrative support. Brewer didn't see eye-to-eye with then-chancellor Gerald Turner, who, according to Brewer, didn't make football a priority. Turner never met with football recruits making official campus visits. He made one exception. After Brewer turned down Turner's request to meet Manning in the chancellor's office Friday afternoon, Turner came to the football office Saturday morning to see Manning.

"I was really upset with that," Brewer said. "He wanted to tell the alumni he had done his pitch on recruiting Peyton."

Brewer made a coaching change that he hoped would not only help his program, but his recruitment of Manning. He hired Larry Kueck as offensive coordinator over Hal Mumme of Valdosta State. Mumme later was hired as Kentucky's head coach before the 1997 season. Kueck would take Ole Miss from the option to the pro-passing attack. But he would do so without Manning.

While Fulmer was the first coach to make a home visit to see the Mannings, Brewer was the last. He went in a week before Manning's scheduled press conference. The hand-writing was on the wall. It was a quiet night. The Mannings didn't ask if Peyton would play as a freshman, or redshirt, or what he needed to work on to get ready.

As he walked from the Mannings' house to his car with Daniels and Kueck, Brewer commented: "He's not coming to Ole Miss."

Brewer was certain of one other thing. Peyton Manning was going to Florida.

"I just didn't think Tennessee was in the picture," Brewer said.

Manning's last recruiting visit was to Florida on Jan. 22-23. He was accompanied by two other prospects from New Orleans: offensive lineman Jarvis Reado and running back Chris Howard. When they arrived in Gainesville, they drove down fraternity row, across the street from Florida Field, where several signs proclaimed, "The Swamp is Peyton's Place."

Howard acted offended. "They really want you," Howard said to Manning. "I wish I could see just one Chris Howard sign, just one." Howard never saw a sign with his name on it. He signed with Michigan.

Reado didn't see a Jarvis Reado sign, either. He signed with Tennessee.

G.A. Mangus, a backup quarterback at Florida in the early 1990s who was a Gators graduate assistant in 1993, helped recruit Manning for Florida.

"Peyton was concerned, and rightly so, about Danny Wuerffel," Mangus said. "Peyton was a very mature kid. He had an agenda. And Peyton wanted to play right away."

He probably wasn't going to do that at Florida. In fact, he might have waited until he was a redshirt junior to play, if he couldn't beat out Wuerffel, an eventual Heisman Trophy winner.

"Lot of people said they thought he didn't want to play for (Florida) coach (Steve) Spurrier," Mangus said. "That was false. At least I never got that. I think Peyton had a lot of respect for coach Spurrier. If Danny wasn't there, who knows what would have happened? But I never felt like we were going to get him because of Wuerffel."

Manning's senior year at Newman, the Southeastern Conference champion Florida Gators played undefeated and No.2-ranked West Virginia in the Sugar Bowl in New Orleans. During the Sugar Bowl game, a Florida fan bought a message on the electronic board: "The Swamp is Peyton's Place." A few seconds later, another message appeared: "No, Ole Miss is Peyton's Place."

The message from the Florida fan reappeared.

Then another message from an Ole Miss fan.

Back and forth they went.

Fans from both schools knew Peyton would be at the Sugar Bowl. Heck, it was a big deal when he went to a Florida practice. *The New Orleans Times-Picayune*, it seemed, wrote as much about Peyton's daily schedule as it did about the Mountaineers that week.

"My gut feeling," Mangus said, "I thought it was Florida/Ole Miss at first. As the weeks went by, I thought it was Florida/Tennessee. Based on the information I was hearing, I thought Ole Miss was a darkhorse."

Randy Sanders thought Florida was out of the picture in January for two reasons. Wuerffel was one factor. Sanders would not elaborate on the other. But, Sanders had two major concerns about luring Manning to Tennessee:

Could Manning say no to Ole Miss?

Would he say yes to Michigan?

Sanders didn't know Manning could say no to Ole Miss until Jan. 25. And the Wolverines were nipping at Manning's heels.

Asked about the recruiting process two months before signing day, Archie Manning said he thought his son would go to Michigan because of Peyton's close relationship with its quarterbacks coach, Cam Cameron.

"Michigan had me scared to death," Sanders said.

If Peyton could say no to Ole Miss, would he compromise and pick Michigan over Tennessee, considering the bitter rivalry between the Vols and Rebels that existed 25 years ago?

"If I went to Ole Miss, the question would be: Can you be as good as your father?" Peyton said. "I could go to Michigan and escape being the son of Archie Manning, SEC legend."

That's what scared Sanders. But Sanders, an underrated cog in Tennessee's recruitment of Manning, felt better and better about Tennessee's chances. On one of his last school visits in January, Sanders went with Manning to a poor-boy eatery in the Garden District. Manning bought Sanders lunch.

Manning was in the process of eliminating Florida and Florida State. He had basically cut Notre Dame, which, like Florida and Florida State, already had a touted freshman quarterback in Ron Powlus. That left Tennessee, Ole Miss and Michigan on the board. It really left Tennessee and Ole Miss, because Manning wasn't going as far north as Ann Arbor, Mich.

Sanders went by Newman another time, but he wasn't scheduled to use one of his three January visits. Manning's girlfriend handed Sanders a personal note written by Manning, saying Peyton was glad Sanders was there.

Archie made just two official recruiting trips with Peyton. One was to Knoxville to visit his former Saints teammate Bobby Scott, and the other was to Michigan because he was doing radio commentary on a Saints game in Cleveland that weekend.

The Mannings visited Tennessee after an ice storm hit Knoxville. Travel was treacherous. After the Mannings departed, Sanders called them that night to make sure they arrived home safely. After talking to Olivia, Sanders felt even better about Tennessee's chances. "I knew we had a great chance to sign him, just reading between the lines," Sanders said.

Sanders never saw Manning play at Newman, but he watched a practice the week before a playoff game. It was cold and rainy. Manning was throwing each pass with zip and accuracy.

Sanders got in his car and immediately phoned Cutcliffe. "This guy could be a great, great player," Sanders told Cutcliffe.

Sanders wasn't the only one sold on Manning. Manning was rated one of the nation's top quarterbacks. He was the Gatorade Circle of Champions national Player of the Year. He was named the high school offensive player of the year by the Columbus (Ohio) Touchdown Club, which twice honored Archie as the college player of the year while he was at Ole Miss.

Manning went to Bill Walsh's quarterback camp at Stanford. Manning was disappointed. He saw Walsh only briefly. After Manning returned to New Orleans, he received a note from a Stanford assistant saying: "Peyton, when you get ready to sign a pro contract, please consider me as your agent. I just want a small percentage."

Washington State coach Mike Price made a hard push, though he knew he had little chance. The Cougars had produced some outstanding quarterbacks in the past 20 years: Jack "The Throwin' Samoan" Thompson, Samoa Samoa, Mark Rypien, Timm Rosenbach, Drew Bledsoe. Three were first-round draft picks and two started for Super Bowl teams.

Price went into Gendusa's office and said: "Frank, I just had to come over here and talk to you. I don't think I have a chance to get Peyton, but I'd hate myself if I didn't come down here and tell you what kind of player I think he is."

Price spent an hour watching film with Gendusa.

"When I look at Peyton on film, he looks like Drew Bledsoe," Price told Gendusa.

Manning could tell you who the Cougars' third-team quarterback was. But he could also tell you he wasn't interested in playing that far from home.

Price didn't land Manning, but he did sign another pretty fair quarterback, Ryan Leaf. Leaf finished third in the 1997 Heisman voting and was the No. 2 overall pick in the 1998 NFL draft.

Notre Dame coach Lou Holtz hoped South Bend, Ind., wasn't too far for Manning. Manning peppered Holtz with a barrage of questions. "I liked that; it meant he had a great deal of interest," Holtz said. "The questions didn't bother me. I was more concerned about the answers I was giving him. I wanted to be truthful and positive."

Shortly after Manning's visit to South Bend, Holtz called Archie: "I've been in this business thirty-something years and I don't think I've had a prospect ask more questions."

One of Manning's questions was about Powlus. "I said, 'Coach Holtz, look me in the eye and tell me where I'm going to be next year,'" Manning asked Holtz.

A month later, Holtz would find out - and it wasn't Notre Dame.

"I felt he'd have fit in at Notre Dame," Holtz said. "One of the most important qualities to be successful at Notre Dame was to be respectful of other people." Yet, during the visit to South Bend, he and brother Cooper playfully mimicked a movie about Notre Dame football that had been recently released, "Rudy." Cooper and Peyton, acting like grade-school kids, ran 15 yards down the tunnel at Notre Dame, jumped up to touch the sign that said, "Play Like a Champion Today," and jogged onto the field like the main character in the film.

"We kept running down the tunnel and onto the field," Cooper said. "We did it over and over."

Newman's Reginelli said Florida State didn't offer Manning a scholarship until two games into Peyton's senior season when the Seminoles realized Manning might be better than Busby. Because FSU was late making an offer, Reginelli suspects Manning questioned how much the Seminoles wanted him.

Manning called FSU quite a bit as a junior. Ronnie Cottrell, then FSU's recruiting coordinator, recalls sitting in the stands with Peyton and Archie Manning watching the Seminoles play a baseball game.

"What a dream," said Cottrell. Soon, the dream went sour.

"I think Peyton liked FSU a lot," Cottrell said. "But when we got a commitment from Thad Busby (the year before), it was over for us."

Cottrell still has a picture of Manning on his official visit to FSU sandwiched between Seminoles quarterbacks: Charlie Ward, Danny Kanell and Busby. Cottrell thought FSU was out of the picture before Manning went to Tallahassee, Fla. "He came out of courtesy because he'd given his word," Cottrell said.

Manning attended Bobby Bowden's camp and left a lasting impression. To this day, Bowden compares all quarterbacks at his camp to Manning and Busby. Three years later, Bowden was lavish in his praise of Manning, calling him one of the best college quarterbacks he'd seen.

"I think you could take Peyton and put him with about 15 different college teams and they'd probably be ranked No. 1," Bowden said during a speaking engagement in Knoxville in the summer of 1997. "I think he's that good."

In January 1994, the family take on Peyton's future was divided. Only Eli thought Peyton was going to Tennessee. Olivia thought it was Ole Miss. Cooper was sure it would be the "Banana Slugs of Santa Cruz or the Hustling Owls of Oregon Tech." Archie said Michigan because Peyton liked the Wolverines' coaches.

Michigan?

Peyton had struck a bond with Cameron. Cameron knew about Manning when Peyton was a sophomore at Newman. In the spring of Peyton's junior season, Cameron took a video camera and taped Manning's practice. It was the first time Cameron had seen Manning in person.

"I still have it to this day," Cameron said. "I took it to Ann Arbor and said, 'This is what we're looking for.'"

Cameron told colleague Fred Jackson on the Michigan staff: "This is the best quarterback I've ever seen (in high school). He's far ahead of anyone mentally."

Cameron says the closest he's seen to Manning since is prep phenom Drew Henson, who signed in February 1998 with Michigan.

"Peyton had the competitiveness of Jim Harbaugh, the toughness of Elvis Grbac, the quick release of Todd Collins, the arm strength of Gus Frerotte, similar athletic ability to Heath Shuler, and he was smarter than any guy I've ever been around at that age," said Cameron, who the year before had the pleasurable experience of recruiting another quarterback with a famous father, Brian Griese.

Brian Griese, son of Bob Greise, walked on at Michigan and eventually led the Wolverines to the 1998 Rose Bowl Championship and a co-national championship. But Brian Griese wasn't a big-time prospect. Peyton Manning was.

Manning made his Michigan visit in December. The frigid weather didn't help Cameron's case.

"In Ann Arbor in December, you might as well be in Alaska," said Cameron. "That's when kids in the South realize they'll be in an element for two months that they've never been in before."

Cameron got enough subtle hints from the Mannings that Peyton probably was going elsewhere. Yet, Michigan was a school that had Tennessee worried. "I knew we were in it, but there was never a point in time I thought we were the school to beat," Cameron said.

While recruiting Manning, Michigan got a commitment from a quarterback from Indiana, Scott Dreisbach. But that's not why Manning didn't sign with Michigan.

"We were a little too far away, and in the wrong conference," Cameron said.

Tennessee was far away, but it was in the right conference.

Tennessee was the right place for another touted high school quarterback. Two days before Manning committed to the Vols, so did Branndon Stewart of Stephenville, Texas.

Fulmer had told Stewart that if he committed to Tennessee, the Vols wouldn't take any more quarterbacks. Fulmer didn't think Tennessee would get Manning. When the Vols did, Fulmer had some explaining to do. Cutcliffe was dispatched to Texas to soothe any ill feelings with the Stewart family. After some soul-searching, Stewart honored his Tennessee commitment.

When told of Manning's commitment, Art Briles, Stewart's high school coach, said: "I don't think it makes any difference. He's a competitor, a great football player. We'll lay the chips on the table and see who's got the best cards."

With that, Briles said he had to take another phone call. Florida's Spurrier was on the line, ready to make a pitch for Stewart. Manning said of Stewart: "He's probably a better quarterback than I am. I wouldn't mind rooming with him."

Said Stewart: "That's a good quote ... I'm sure it'll be a great experience."

Manning said he was disappointed Shuler turned pro early because he would have liked to play behind, "A great quarterback for a year." Manning added: "I'm going to go in there humble. I might be No. 10 on the depth chart. I know I'll have to earn my way. ... Obviously the jump from Newman is going to be huge."

As for Ole Miss, Manning said on the day he committed to Tennessee: "No matter what I would have done, I'd never have been as good as the people in Mississippi think I am."

Said Archie: "The Ole Miss side of me is disappointed, but the daddy part is excited."

At a young age, a Manning trait surfaced. He sought the advice of key people when it came to making important decisions. No decision in his life, at the time, was as important as choosing a college.

Manning met with Dr. Leavell, then an interim pastor at the Manning's church and president of the New Orleans Baptist Seminary.

"He asked me to pray with him about his decision," said Leavell, now retired and living in Wichita Falls, Texas. "He was struggling. He didn't want to do the wrong thing.

"I told him, 'The decision is yours, you will make the right one, I know you, I believe in you.'"

Leavell said Peyton's visit was unexpected but not surprising. "He was that kind of lad," Leavell said. "He knew the decision was so important, he couldn't afford to make a mistake."

The meeting was in January 1994. Peyton had narrowed his choices to Tennessee, Ole Miss and Notre Dame, Leavell said.

"I said, 'It's really down to two; you ain't going to Notre Dame,'" Leavell said.

Leavell was right. Manning wasn't going to Notre Dame. But would it be Ole Miss or Tennessee?

Leavell said Peyton didn't express concern about following in his father's footsteps to Ole Miss, nor did he express concern about the flak Archie would take if Peyton rejected the Rebels.

"He told me his father said, 'Whatever you decide, I'll back you.' He didn't fear what his daddy might think or do."

Leavell derived from his chat with Manning that Tennessee was the school.

"He told me Ole Miss if Cooper was still playing," Leavell said. "That pretty well eliminated Ole Miss. He said he'd been to Tennessee and liked what he saw very much, he liked the system, the facilities, everything he'd seen.'"

Leavell wasn't surprised Peyton picked Tennessee, but he was a little disappointed. Leavell's father played football at Ole Miss.

"From a sentimental standpoint," Leavell said, "I would have loved to see him put Ole Miss back on the football map."

Curiosity hit the Crescent City when Archie's two sons, Cooper (No. 18) and Peyton (No. 14) played at Isidore Newman High School in the early 1990s.

Chapter Three:

The Making of Manning

"You don't see a player like Peyton Manning come through but once in a lifetime"

– Tony Reginelli
Newman coach

IF YOU DIDN'T GET A CHANCE TO SEE THE sixth-grade intramural flag football championship game at Newman School in 1987, you missed quite a show.

Little Peyton Manning, he of the skinny legs and rail-thin arms, was flinging the ball all over the field. He passed his team to a 35-7 lead. Then with less than a minute left, he called time-out.

"Peyton," said his intramural coach, Bradley "Butch" Farris, "why did you call time-out?"

"I don't know coach," Manning said. "I was thinking, 'What should I run here?'"

"Peyton," Farris said, "we're up 35-7. We don't need to do anything spectacular. Just run the ball. A little handoff here and the game is over. Just call a play and let's see how you do."

Manning called a play all right. Leading by 28 points with less than a minute left, the rogue in Manning told him it was time for a double-reverse pass. Touchdown.

"Coach," Manning said, "do you think that was a little bit too much?"

If Peyton Manning was conservative off the field, he was liberal on the field. He was razzle dazzle. He was flash. He was go-for-broke. At age

11, Air Manning had arrived.

Fast forward six years. Newman High School has never won a state championship in football, never reached the state finals. The Greenies are in the second round of the Class AA playoffs at Northeast High School in Zachary, coached by former Super Bowl quarterback Doug Williams. A Northeast punt rolls dead at the Newman 1-yard line. Newman trails by less than a touchdown.

Manning starts to jog onto the field, then retreats. He has an idea. He tells offensive coordinator Frank Gendusa he wants to run a naked bootleg. Gendusa almost has a coronary. A naked bootleg from your own 1-yard line when you're behind in the state quarterfinals?

"Peyton, we're on the 1-yard line," Gendusa explains.

"Yeah, coach, but that end has been coming hard," Manning says.

Gendusa relents, with one stipulation: "Send out one receiver so if you get stuck, you can dump the ball off so we don't get a safety."

Manning fakes a handoff; he runs the naked bootleg. The defensive end takes the fake, but quickly recovers. Manning can see him coming; knows he's caught. Manning stops. He flicks a 15-yard pass to his receiver, Chip Abbott, the state 100-meter champion. No one catches Abbott. Touchdown.

Against rival Buras, Newman has the ball and a 14-0 lead late in the second quarter. Head coach Tony Reginelli wants to run out the clock and take a two-touchdown cushion into halftime. Manning and Gendusa aren't so patient. Gendusa calls for the two-minute offense. Boom. Boom. Boom. Boom. Four plays and 68 seconds later, Newman is ahead 21-0.

Reginelli isn't satisfied. He turns to Gendusa and snarls: "You left too much time on the clock."

Spectacular plays were commonplace for Manning at Newman. They started at a young age and continued through a brilliant career that brought national attention to this elite school near the Garden District of New Orleans. Newman was founded in 1903 as a manual training school for Jewish orphans. Today, it is considered one of the nation's top academic high schools. It has 1,100 students in grades k-through-12. Its athletic programs are highly successful, annually contending for the

Class AA all-sports trophy in Louisiana. In the 1997-98 school year, Newman won two state titles and had four runner-up finishes. Its football staff has two coaches who were recently head coaches at other high schools.

Tuition is about $10,000 per year (not counting books) for grades 9-12. Freshmen pay a little more because they take a field trip to Washington, D.C. To be admitted, you must take a test at age 3-and-a-half that indicates whether you can handle the difficult curriculum. Out of a recent graduating class of 80 students, 20 went to Ivy League schools.

Newman has a storied history, but it had seen nothing like what happened during the Manning years. First was Cooper, a star receiver who played on two state championship teams in basketball. Then came Peyton, two years younger, a three-sport athlete who brought national acclaim with an article in *Sports Illustrated* his senior season. Then came Eli, five years younger than Peyton and a national recruit entering his senior season in 1998.

Curiosity hit the Crescent City in the late 1980s.

"People got curious at the seventh-grade level because word got out that Archie's sons were playing on Newman's teams," said Claude "Boo" Mason, Newman's athletic director for 19 years (1977-96). "But none of the boys were as athletic as Archie."

Archie Manning was an All-Pro quarterback for the New Orleans Saints. He was an All-American quarterback at Ole Miss. He was a gifted shortstop who was twice drafted by the major leagues. He is respected as much as a person as he is for his athletic ability. He was considered a saint off the field because, despite playing for a morbid franchise, he never complained and never pointed an accusing finger. New Orleans never had a more popular athlete.

Then, along came his sons. Would they be as good athletically as Archie? Would their characters be cut from the same cloth as Archies'? New Orleans was curious.

"Being here when Peyton was playing was kind of a vicarious kick," Newman principal Bill Andrews said. "You liked being there. You liked some of the reflected glory: 'You're the principal at Newman; that's where Peyton Manning plays.' All the sudden, you're elevated in the eyes of other people just by happenstance."

Cooper played some quarterback initially at Newman. His first snap, as a sophomore, was a 99-yard bootleg pass to Omar Douglas, today a receiver for the New York Giants. Cooper moved to wide receiver exclusively as a junior. He eventually followed his father's footsteps and signed to play at Ole Miss. "Cooper was one of the best possession receivers I ever coached," Gendusa said.

Peyton was a quarterback from the get-go. He wasn't about to try any other position. Archie was a quarterback, and by gosh, Peyton would be one, too.

"Peyton ran the option pretty good in the seventh grade," Reginelli said. "Peyton wanted to be a runner. He'd seen enough film of his dad, and his dad was a tremendous runner."

The Manning kids weren't allowed to play organized tackle football until the seventh grade. Archie didn't believe in starting any younger. "It's a bad idea — too dangerous," he said. Once Peyton reached seventh grade, his quarterback traits were evident, said Mason, Peyton's first football coach. By the end of that season, Manning was calling his own plays.

"You could see those leadership skills and that competitiveness and intensity. It was wonderful," said Mason, who had the distinction of being around two No. 1 overall picks in the National Football League. Peyton was the No. 1 pick of the 1998 draft. Mason's younger brother, Tommy, a former halfback at Tulane, was the No. 1 overall pick in 1960 by the Minnesota Vikings, the first player ever selected by that franchise.

"Cooper loved to compete, too, but I didn't see the same level of intensity in Cooper that I saw in Peyton," Mason said. Even so, Mason's observation wasn't evident when the brothers competed against each other. Their back-yard basketball games turned into basket-brawls. Fisticuffs were common. Peyton, a chunky momma's boy as a youth, always cried.

"He was kind of a baby," mother Olivia Manning said. "Peyton liked to tell on Cooper."

"Fake tears," Cooper said of Peyton.

Claude "Boo" Mason was Peyton Manning's coach in the seventh grade, Peyton's first year of organized football. Mason not only coached an eventual No. 1 draft choice in the NFL, his brother Tommy was the No. 1 overall pick in the 1960 NFL draft.

The tears might have been fake. The fights weren't.

"They fought like cats and dogs," Olivia said. "It scared me to death. If I was home with them and they'd start playing basketball, I'd almost want to get a broom or a (water) hose to separate them."

During the state basketball finals in 1992, Newman's star player, Randy Livingston, got into foul trouble late in the first half. Peyton Manning replaced him with one minute and a few seconds left. The opposing fans began a countdown — "four...three...two...one" - and Peyton fell for it. With more than one minute left, he launched a shot from the back court that caromed off the shot-clock above the basket. Peyton's face turned crimson. He was flustered. Cooper wasn't sympathetic. As if they were in the backyard again, Cooper started screaming at his younger brother.

"What the hell are you doing?" Cooper yelled.

Peyton Manning: Primed and Ready

Nate Hibbs, one of Peyton's best receivers at Newman, said Manning didn't take basketball as seriously as he took football. So, rather than brood about the incident, Hibbs said, "He laughed about it more than we did."

The sibling spats carried over to football. Peyton was a demanding quarterback. He expected perfection from himself and his teammates. During a game in 1991, Peyton threw a pass low and away. Cooper couldn't catch it. Peyton was furious. He walked downfield and let Cooper have it.

"If Cooper didn't come up with grass and dirt on his face mask, Peyton would meet him two yards downfield and tell him he didn't make a good enough effort," Reginelli said. "I'd tell Peyton, 'You can't yell at receivers like that.' And he'd say, 'Coach, the ball was catchable.' And I'd say, 'That's a senior; that's your brother, too.'"

Senior, brother, teammate. Peyton Manning didn't care. He wanted to win, and he thought everyone should want to win as much as he did. He was demanding of his teammates. "The thing I think he learned from us was, everybody's not as gifted as you are, everybody's not as talented as you are, everybody's not as dedicated as you are," Gendusa said. "You have to understand those levels and adjust. You're not necessarily going to make an average player into a great player, but you can make him into a player who gives you his best."

When Manning was a sophomore, Gendusa turned to Cooper to help chill Peyton. "I think Peyton made great strides in that from his sophomore year to his senior year."

"You can't let it upset you when you throw the ball on the money and the guy drops it," Gendusa told Peyton. "It's all part of the game. You still have to play with that wide receiver after he dropped the ball, because he's the best kid we have in there.

"Peyton realized that. I think it became a non-issue his junior and senior year."

Well, not exactly. Hibbs said the perfectionist in Manning often surfaced.

"If we didn't run the right route," Hibbs said, "he'd go down field and let you know. At the time, you might not like it. But after the game, you were thankful. He wanted us to be as successful as he was. He was very committed. He was like a coach on the field."

How did the players handle Manning's outbursts?

"You're always going to have some friction," said Hibbs, one of the few Greenies who would tell Manning to take a hike if he thought Manning was carrying things too far. "There were some disagreements, but nothing lingered on." Said halfback Cameron Johnson: "He'd definitely jump on you."

Manning, it seemed, had forgotten a family rule: It's better to be a good person than a good player. "It wasn't happening that much," Archie said. "But Peyton, at times, was being a jerk. I had to get tough with him. I told him we wouldn't tolerate it. It is one thing to compete; it is another thing to have some class. He is just serious as a heart attack about sports and everyone else isn't as committed, and he had to understand that."

However, receiver/defensive back Baldwin Montgomery said Manning's fiery nature elevated Newman's football team.

"We had some talent, but he definitely brought us to another level," Montgomery said. "I've known all my life he was a special player. He has the most incredible work ethic of anybody I ever met in my life. And he was gifted enough to be born with raw talent." Montgomery said Manning was careful to make sure cameras weren't around when he chastised teammates.

Did any player resent it?

"I didn't," Montgomery said. "Some people may have. ... But you know if you did something wrong, you've got to take it. Heck, he'd get after his brother, too."

Said Hibbs: "He didn't like to kid around, even if we were up five or six touchdowns."

To Manning, it was all about competing, all about winning. That's why he got after his teammates. That's why he studied film for hours. That's why he'd start practice at Newman 15 minutes before the coaches arrived.

That's why one night after he'd played a baseball game, he went to the

Newman head coach Tony Reginelli called Peyton Manning "a once in a lifetime player."

darkened football field at Newman and ran sprints with special shoes that were supposed to increase your speed. Reginelli happened to be in his office near the stadium after returning from a girls softball game.

"The lights are out, it's dark, and you hear somebody running, you see a blur go by the window," Reginelli said. "I wondered, 'Who in the heck is that? Who would be running at this time of night?'"

The mystery man ran several 100-yard sprints and was huffing and puffing before Reginelli figured it out. "Peyton, is that you?" Reginelli yelled.

"Yes coach, I've got to do some extra running to work on my speed and conditioning. These defensive linemen, they can run 4.7, 4.8. I got to get up there."

"Hell, what are you doing? You could hit a bump or a hole and pull a hamstring."

"No, coach, I'll be OK. I've been doing it pretty often."

Incidents like that caused Reginelli to marvel at Manning's work ethic. "You couldn't work him hard enough," Reginelli said. "You might beat him but you will never out-prepare him. It goes back to this: great athletes will work on their weakness."

That greatness wasn't evident to everyone. Asked if he knew as a high school freshman that Manning would be a star college quarterback, Hibbs said: "Absolutely not. We were just hitting puberty and growing at the same rate. He always had a great feel for the game, but he was kind of awkward and had a goofy look. His body couldn't grasp how fast he was growing."

Manning was a marked man at Newman. Everyone knew who he was. Everyone knew how good he was, or was supposed to be. The 1,250 seats at Newman High School often overflowed with fans. At the playoff game in Zachary against Northeast, about 3,000 fans lined the fences of a stadium that seated 1,000.

"With the Mannings, Friday nights around here were exciting," Farris said. "When we'd travel, the crowds would come. Everybody was out gunning for Peyton. I remember one time somebody sacked Peyton. You'd have thought the kid had won a gold medal in the Olympics. He was jumping up and cheering. That's the only thing he wanted to do in the game - sack Peyton."

Manning might have been born to play quarterback, but he wasn't spoon-fed. Clearly, he earned everything he achieved.

"I've been here 17 years and no one has worked harder than Peyton

Manning on the field, in the class room or the weight room," Gendusa said. "He's always gone the extra yard or extra mile. He's going to do whatever it takes to be the best possible person and player he can be. He has worked for whatever he is."

During the heat of the summer, Newman School had day camps. Several football players worked the camps. Manning would recruit the receivers who were working at the camps and throw to them in 98-degree heat and humidity during lunch breaks.

"What are you doing in this heat?" Reginelli asked.

"Coach," Manning said. "We've got to play in this weather; we've got to get used to it."

Manning was so driven, he made sure his classes were over at 2:30 p.m. his senior season at Newman so he could go to Tulane's campus or the Saints' facility and throw to receivers during 7-on-7 drills.

"Peyton would sneak out there on his own," Reginelli said. "He got in as much work as he could."

Peyton Manning impressed former Saints quarterback Jim Everett and All-Pro defender Pat Swilling. One day, Reginelli asked Everett about Manning's ability, release and arm strength.

"Coach," Everett said, "he can play with anybody right now."

That, in all likelihood, included the Saints.

"He was a better passer than anybody the Saints had," said former Ole Miss coach Billy Brewer. "I'm not kidding. He'd been programmed. He was a robot."

The most enjoyable year of Peyton Manning's football career came during his sophomore season at Newman. He completed 140 passes, 75 to Cooper. Once, on the sideline, a television camera captured the Mannings and Gendusa drawing up a play in the sand. Gendusa solicited the Mannings' input because players often see things that aren't noticeable from the sideline.

"When you have kids like the Mannings who are football wise, you'd be stupid not to get some feedback," Gendusa said. "I don't think we drew up 100 plays, but we definitely made adjustments."

Peyton Manning put up remarkable numbers at Newman. As a senior, he completed 168 of 265 passes for 2,703 yards and 39 touchdowns. As a junior, he hit 144 of 264 for 2,345 yards and 30 TDs. As a sophomore, he was 140 of 230 for 2,142 yards and 23 scores. His career totals: 452 of 761 for 7,207 yards and 92 touchdowns. He also rushed for 338 yards and 13 touchdowns, accounting for 105 scores in his career.

"You don't see a player like Peyton Manning come through but once in a lifetime," Reginelli said.

Manning's marks likely will remain in the Newman record books for years, unless they are broken by Peyton's younger brother, Eli. Unlike the fiery and assertive Peyton, Eli is laid back. Otherwise, their similarities are astounding. Peyton was 6 foot 5 inches and 195 pounds his senior season at Newman. Eli was 6 foot 4 inches and 190 entering his senior season. As a sophomore, Eli had more passing yards (2,340) and touchdown passes (26) than Peyton. As a junior, Eli passed for 2,547 yards - eclipsing Peyton's total by 202 yards - and 24 scores - six fewer than his older brother.

Newman went 34-5 in Peyton Manning's three years as a starter: 12-2 as a sophomore, 11-2 as a junior, 11-1 as a senior. Three losses were in the state playoffs. In the 10th grade, Manning threw a last-minute interception in a 16-14 loss to Haynesville in the semifinals. The next year, a foreign exchange student from Spain kicked a 43-yard field goal in the finals seconds as Pickering upset Newman in the quarterfinals. As a senior, Manning passed for 396 yards, but the Greenies lost at Northeast of Zachary in the second round.

Gendusa said he knew Manning was special in the third grade, the way he was focused and competed even while playing kids' games. It showed up on the football field in later years. In a junior varsity game as a freshman, Manning looked at his primary receiver over the middle, the safety came up, then Manning threw a 40-yard bullet over the stunned safety's head for a 70-yard score.

In another freshman game, Manning led Newman to scores running a no-huddle, two-minute drill *twice* in the last two minutes of the first half.

If anyone breaks Peyton Manning's career passing records at Newman High School, it will be younger brother Eli Manning (above), who bears a strong resemblance to his brother at the same stage of their careers.

"Right then you knew what kind of athlete you had on your hands," said junior varsity coach Jeff Brock. Manning had a unique ability at a young age to understand sophisticated secondary coverages that are common on the varsity or college level, Brock said. "He wanted to know what people were doing and how to be able to identify it when the ball was snapped."

"This is a young man who ate most of the meals of his life across the table from an all-pro quarterback. So obviously something is going to rub off very early. When we played other teams, coaches were in awe at how sophisticated he was at 14, how well he threw the ball, how accurate he was, the quick-strike capability."

Cooper wore No. 18 at Newman, the same number that his father wore at Ole Miss. Peyton wore No. 14 as a sophomore, the same number his father wore in high school. But midway during his junior season, Peyton switched to 18. There was a good reason.

Cooper experienced numbness in his right hand during his senior season at Newman. He complained that his hand was cold, even on warm nights. He went to Saints team orthopedic physician Terry Habig, who recommended ulnar-nerve surgery in his right elbow. Cooper later played in the Louisiana high school all-star game and went through two-a-days at Ole Miss. He made the Rebels' traveling squad, but the numbness returned.

Something was seriously wrong.

Cooper went for treatment at the Mayo Clinic in Minnesota and the Baylor Medical Center in Dallas. Doctors discovered Cooper had a narrowing of the spinal canal. He could never play football again. It was a miracle he'd made it through high school without serious injury. A doctor at Tulane University said if he'd taken an X-ray of Cooper's neck in the fourth grade, Cooper would have never played football.

The news was bittersweet. Cooper's football-playing days were over, but at least he hadn't incurred a serious injury, and at least he got to enjoy playing football with his brother in high school. Saddened by the news, Peyton Manning changed his number from 14 to 18. Cooper sent Peyton a touching letter about his situation. It said, in part: "I would like to live my dream of playing football through you. Although I cannot play anymore, I know I can still get the same feeling out of watching my little brother do what he does best. I know now that we are good for each other, because I need you to be serious and look at things from a different perspective. I am good for you, as well, to take things light. I love you, Peyt, and only great things lay ahead for you. Thanks for everything on and off the field."

Cooper would play — vicariously — through his younger brother. And Peyton would learn a valuable lesson: football isn't forever.

"When you grow up in New Orleans in the Manning house, football is important to you," Peyton said. "For doctors to say, 'Cooper, your career is over,' like that, it was tough for him. I thought that's the least I could do, changing to his number.

"It made me realize my next play could be my last play."

He also realized football was his ticket, but he was good at baseball and basketball.

Manning played shortstop and hit .440 as a junior, leading his team to the state finals. After a slow start as a senior, he got hot and carried his team during the playoffs. He had good range and an excellent arm.

Newman baseball coach Billy Fitzgerald said he thought Manning could have been a major college prospect as a third baseman. Fitzgerald would have liked for Manning to pitch, but Manning never showed an interest.

Foreshadowing his slight of hand as a quarterback, Manning was adept at the hidden-ball trick in baseball. He would fake a throw back to the pitcher and stick the ball under his left armpit. He would show his glove and hand to the base runner to lure him off the bag, then tag him out.

"We had great fun with that," Fitzgerald said.

But Manning did have some failures in baseball. As a 15-year-old during Babe Ruth summer league, he had trouble fielding the ball, prompting his coach, Slade Simons, to write "E-6" on the equipment bag.

"Peyton didn't like it one bit," Montgomery said. "I don't know if he said anything to the coach, but we loved it. We didn't let him live it down."

In basketball, Manning was the backup point guard to Livingston, one of the finest high school players in Louisiana history. Livingston carried Newman to three straight Class AA state titles.

At the start of his junior season in basketball, Manning and Fitzgerald, who also coached basketball, got crossways. Ever the competitor, Manning wanted to play more. Fitzgerald, who some said didn't like the idea of football players joining the team late, didn't yield.

Mason tried to play peacemaker. Even as he talked about it five years later, he was close to tears.

Mason, Newman's A.D., called Manning into his office and asked Manning if he thought he was a team player. Manning said, yes. It was an uncomfortable meeting. "I was asking to force a response," Mason said, his voice shaky. "I thought he needed to think about what was his role on that particular team at that particular time."

Fitzgerald, who has won five state championships, acknowledged the dispute, but said he couldn't recall exact details. "I basically attributed it to the fact that Peyton was a great competitor," Fitzgerald said. "He wanted to be in there in the thick of things. I didn't agree on his assessment that he should have been in at that time. We had a disagreement and it probably influenced him into putting basketball behind him and moving on." Manning quit basketball shortly after meeting with Mason.

The wedge that developed between Manning and Fitzgerald did not carry over to baseball. Manning played baseball for four years under Fitzgerald. Fitzgerald had an appreciation for Manning's tenacity.

"He's a great competitor," Fitzgerald said. "That is easily one of his greatest strengths. He doesn't tolerate anything but the absolute best from himself and his teammates and he expects the best from himself and his teammates."

Peyton Manning is not so intense away from sports. Reginelli remembers the time Newman won a playoff game at Kentwood on a tipped pass that was caught by Julian Billings. On the return trip to New Orleans, one of the two team buses broke down on I-55.

"We were on the interstate and couldn't get off the bus," Reginelli said.

"Peyton entertained the whole group for 45 minutes. He put in a tape and he and Cooper starting singing into the P.A. system."

If you're looking for the Manning Achilles' heel, look no farther than their voices.

"Cooper and Peyton can't sing, not a lick," Brock said. "They think they can. They think they're good. But they were terrible. They were the worst singers. Unless Peyton has taken a lot of voice lessons, he's still bad."

Johnson said Manning was a cut-up away from athletics and academics. He liked to drink a few beers and he wasn't beyond practical jokes. "He was always fun to go out with," Johnson said. "I could listen to his stories for an hour and crack up the whole time. He was very humorous and loved to play jokes on people. He definitely could let everything loose and have fun."

Manning was a good student. He maintained a 3.5 grade-point average at a tough school. He scored 23 on the American College Test and 1030 on the Scholastic Aptitude Test. "He wasn't naturally brilliant, but he put his time in and worked for what he got," said Johnson, a Southern Methodist University graduate who drove 13 hours - from Dallas to Athens, Ga. — to see Manning play against Georgia in 1996.

Manning's senior year, he took calculus from Dr. Sheila Collins.

"The thing I remember most about the class," Collins recalled, "is that it was one of the nicest classes I ever had. I remarked that to other faculty members and they said probably one of the reasons was the fact Peyton was in the class because he has such a positive effect on other students. I thought that was a nice compliment.

"He was always a positive person, never negative. If he didn't do something, he always said, 'I didn't do it.' He didn't blame. A lot of kids will blame everybody, including the dog, but he never did that. He was always very up front. If he didn't do something, he'd say, 'I'm sorry, I didn't do it,' and take whatever the consequences were. He was really a delightful person to have in your class."

Manning sat in the back of the class so he wouldn't obstruct the view of smaller students.

That type consideration filtered from his father, who showed similar

Newman coach Frank Gendusa said it's been a privilege to coach the Manning boys. Gendusa admits he drew up plays in the dirt when Peyton and Cooper played together at Newman.

sensitivity to his sons' coaches by never interfering.

"My dad doesn't get involved," Peyton said. "That's his policy. I appreciated that so much. That's why he's a good father."

Archie didn't talk football with Newman's coaches unless they asked. Reginelli did ask - once. He invited Archie over to discuss the passing system Newman was about to install. Reginelli and Gendusa said they never felt intimidated by coaching Archie's son. They knew Archie would leave them alone, and they knew he would be respectful and

73

supportive of their decisions.

"I felt privileged to coach his sons," Gendusa said.

Peyton was so advanced at a young age, he would, as Reginelli said, make the coaches look good. He also kept them sharp. Saturday morning after a Friday night game, Manning would knock on the coaches' door wanting to know the pass coverages of next week's opponents.

"We're just getting rid of one game, and already he's on top of you before you start looking at the scouting report," Reginelli said. "You had to be prepared."

Naturally, Peyton Manning is a favorite alum of Newman. An area in the archives' section of the school is called "Peyton's Alley." It has clips, photos, a life-size Manning poster and other memorabilia about Manning's career at Tennessee. Two huge portable backboards display stories about Manning and his family. Want to know how popular Peyton Manning is at Newman? The school had a Parents Association Fund-raiser on April 19, 1998. One item was an autographed jacket from actor Bruce Willis. Another was a Peyton Manning autographed jersey from a Citrus Bowl game.

The Willis jacket went for $700.

The Manning jersey went for over $2,100.

Manning brought Newman to a new level in football, Gendusa said. Newman had been competitive in football, but with Manning, the Greenies were a threat to win the state championship.

"We were good enough to win if we got a few breaks," Gendusa said. "I think he took us to that level and we've been there since."

In 1997, Newman had a school-record 90 players out for football of 225 boys in grades 9-12.

"He did bring an awareness of football to this school, to himself, to our team," Gendusa said.

"It was a treat coaching him. It's something every coach hopes comes around one time in his coaching career. You're not only dealing with a fine athlete, but a really great person with extraordinary character and leadership abilities. He had it all."

Newman High School is proud of its most famous graduate. An archives section of the school is called Peyton's Alley because of all the photos and clippings of Peyton's career.

Peyton Manning is the epitome of poise and composure now. But he was quickly humbled by his offensive linemen when he went into the huddle for the first game of his college career.

Chapter Four:

A Star is Born

"Shut the * @%! up and call the play."
– Tennessee offensive
lineman Jason Layman

NO. 16 TROTTED INTO THE TENNESSEE HUDDLE. IT was in the Rose Bowl on national television, against Terry Donahue's UCLA Bruins. His parents squirmed in their end-zone seats.

"You've gotta be kidding!," they thought.

Peyton Manning wasn't supposed to play against UCLA in the season opener. He wasn't supposed to play in 1994, period, except maybe in a mop up role. The Vols had a fifth-year senior quarterback, Jerry Colquitt, who had patiently waited his turn to start. They had a junior from Knoxville who doubled as a baseball star, Todd Helton. Manning and Branndon Stewart were two highly touted quarterback prospects signed in February 1994, but neither figured to make an immediate mark. They might take a few snaps. But more than likely they would redshirt, then battle for the starting job in 1995. That was the game plan.

So much for game plans.

On the seventh play of the UCLA game, Colquitt tore the anterior cruciate ligament in his right knee while running an option play. He would be lost for the season. Helton, who would be named the 1995 college baseball Player of the Year nine months later, was unexpectedly thrust into action. He didn't play well. After three series, Tennessee had not scored a point. And those three first downs Helton engineered didn't satisfy offensive coordinator David Cutcliffe.

The television camera panned the Tennessee sideline, finding Manning.

"There's one pair of sweaty palms right there," said ABC-TV announcer Keith Jackson.

Earlier that day, Manning talked via telephone with his grandfather Cooper Williams, in Philadelphia, Miss. Peyton was studying Tennessee's playbook, just in case.

When Williams asked if Peyton would play, Peyton said: "You never know."

Williams: "I bet you'll play."

Archie Manning couldn't believe his son's optimism: "You're not going to play, Peyton," he said.

The backdrop of mountains surrounded the storied and historic Rose Bowl. Jackson squinted to read those orange numbers against a white jersey. And suddenly, by fate, here was Peyton Manning, warming up on the sidelines after Colquitt's injury.

"I still remember the look on Peyton's face when I said, 'Get your arm loose,'" Tennessee coach Phillip Fulmer said. Instead of warming up his arm, he warmed up his legs.

"I was shaking," Manning said. "My heart started pounding. They said, 'Peyton, get on the (head) phones, you're going in.' I'll never forget those words.

"I can remember doing sprints on the sideline, just trying to get loose. It's probably as fast as I've ever run around here."

Then, Manning took the field. Jackson squinted again. Was that really No. 16?

"Here comes Peyton Manning making his entry as the quarterback for the University of Tennessee," Jackson bellowed. "Get used to it."

It was hard for Olivia Manning to get used to it. "He looks so young out there," said Peyton's mother.

Young or not, Peyton Manning was ready to conquer the world. He marched into the huddle with the swagger of Joe Namath and boasted confidently to his teammates: "I know I'm just a freshman, but I can lead us down field for a touchdown."

Are you serious? This young pup was giving a pep talk to a bunch of grizzled veterans who were getting their collective butts kicked. They weren't in the mood. Tackle Jason Layman grabbed Manning by the jersey and snarled: "Shut the *@%! up and call the play."

Manning was stunned. Wasn't the quarterback supposed to take control in the huddle? Wasn't the quarterback the leader? Wasn't he the take-charge guy? That's what his dad had always told him.

Then you get some hairy-faced, 310-pound lineman in your face, cursing you right there in front of nine other guys.

"He hadn't earned their respect at that particular time," said Fulmer.

No kidding. Manning had practiced with the varsity for one month.

"They humbled me so quickly," Manning said of the offensive linemen. "I said, 'OK' and called the play."

The after-effects were lengthy. "I said nothing extra in the huddle for the next eight games," Manning said.

On Manning's first collegiate play, he handed off to tailback James Stewart, who gained nine yards. On second down, a run up the middle was stuffed for no gain. On third down, guard Kevin Mays told Manning to hurry to the line of scrimmage because UCLA's defense wasn't set. Manning did as ordered. You wouldn't want another 300-pounder on your butt, either.

UCLA's defense wasn't set, but neither was Tennessee's offense. Not all of the linemen were in their stance when Manning barked the signals. They charged off the line at different times, totally out of sync. No gain again. On his first college series, Manning was cursed at, ordered around, humbled and left empty-handed. He went three-and-out against UCLA - and never returned.

Some debut.

"Three plays? What's the deal?" he asked Cutcliffe after the game.

If Cutcliffe hadn't been so shell-shocked at losing Colquitt for the rest of the season, he might have grabbed Manning's jersey, too. Who was this freshman who was whining about playing time after his first game? Who was this Opie-looking kid who was complaining after the Vols made a marvelous rally from an 18-0 deficit to lose 25-23 behind a spirited second-half performance from Helton? Who did this skinny, 198-pound weakling think he was?

Well, he thought he was as ready as any other healthy quarterback on the roster.

"I was hungry," Manning said. "I wanted to play."

Peyton Manning arrived in Knoxville in July of 1994, five months after signing a national letter of intent with Tennessee. He came to get acclimated academically. He came to get acclimated socially. But most of all, he came to compete. He said he wouldn't mind redshirting as a freshman, then trying to win the starting job in 1995.

Maybe so. But deep in the recesses of his mind, a voice told him to be prepared. He'd seen his father come home, belted and bruised after playing games for the New Orleans Saints. If he learned anything from his father, he learned a backup could be just a play away from becoming a starter. So he prepared.

Manning grabbed headlines before he actually reported to Tennessee, when he threw to several pro receivers during the summer. Not only were the New Orleans Saints' receivers impressed, but Saints outside linebacker Pat Swilley said Manning looked like he was ready for the NFL. After *The Knoxville News-Sentinel* ran a wire story in which the Saints were complimenting Manning, Fulmer called the paper, concerned that Branndon Stewart might be offended at not getting equal treatment. That was a precursor of the way Fulmer would delicately try to coddle Stewart and handle what would develop into a heated quarterback debate.

If nothing else, Manning was determined to be ready mentally.

In May of 1994, Cutcliffe visited the Mannings in New Orleans. Cutcliffe explained Tennessee's offense to Peyton. "Peyton was eating it up," Cutcliffe said. Archie wasn't. He fell asleep.

The mental Manning was far ahead of the physical Manning. "I was worried about my physical stature," said Peyton Manning. "What if I had to bench press in front of the other players? I was afraid of that."

Manning's boney body could bench press about 220 pounds. Branndon

Stewart, a high school weight-lifting champion with a sculptured physique, was in the 350 range. Stewart also had a stronger arm. Archie's fatherly advice: Work as hard as you can and don't worry about how much you bench press in front of your teammates.

For Manning to beat out Stewart for the number three quarterback job, he would have to watch film. He would have to learn the playbook. He would have to outwork and outthink his counterpart.

A few days after Manning moved to Knoxville in the summer of 1994, he tracked down Tennessee trainer Mike Rollo for access to a film room.

"It was a Sunday in July," Rollo recalled. "Athletes don't do this sort of thing. They can find 70 other things to do besides watching somebody else's games. He was a student of the game since he got here.

"If Peyton Manning and Heath Shuler had come here at the same time, probably the same thing would have happened. Peyton would have been the starter. Heath worked at it physically, but not anywhere near the way Peyton worked at it mentally."

During the summer months, coaches aren't allowed to help players. So Manning left a crack in the film-room door so the coaches knew he was studying. "I wasn't trying to brown-nose the coaches," Manning said. "But I wanted them to know what I was doing."

Said Cutcliffe: "He was going to do the effort thing."

One day, Stewart asked Manning to watch film with him. Manning said he couldn't. Then, when they left the football facility, Manning ducked back over to the Neyland-Thompson Sports Center to watch more film. "I wanted to get an edge," Manning said.

Such was Manning's competitive nature.

While Stewart left Knoxville in late July to play in the Texas high school all-star game in Houston, Manning declined an invitation to play in the Louisiana high school all-star game so he could study UT's playbook, study more film. He was always looking for that edge. In October, when the battle was heating up, Cutcliffe had his regular 6 p.m. quarterback meeting. Cutcliffe is a stickler for promptness. At 6 sharp, Manning was sitting in the film room with Cutcliffe. Stewart wasn't there.

"It's one minute past six, and no Branndon," Cutcliffe said. "I'm mad. I

Peyton was so insecure about his bench press, he was worried about lifting weights in front of his new Tennessee teammates. Four years later, Manning bench pressed 335 pounds.

said, 'Where in the world is Branndon?'"

Manning gave an innocent shrug.

An angry Cutcliffe stomped off, looking for Stewart.

The building is locked on Sunday's, so Cutcliffe, who had a key, would leave an object to keep the door from locking so the quarterbacks could enter. After Manning came in, he shut the door, knocking away the prop to lock Stewart out. Cutcliffe eventually found Stewart, outside the building.

"When I went back up in the (meeting) room, there's this guy sitting down with a grin on his face," Cutcliffe said. "He never said anything about it. That's the kind of competitor Peyton Manning is. He locked Branndon out of the building to make him late."

Tennessee coaches had never seen anyone so diligent in the film room, especially not a true freshman.

"He absorbed things like a sponge," Cutcliffe said. "He has remarkable recall." His recall was such that one Tennessee coach nicknamed him R2D2, after the robot in the *Star Wars* movies.

Helton didn't pay as much attention as Manning. He daydreamed about home runs and stolen bases. But when Manning took to answering questions directed at Helton, Helton got irritated.

"Damn it, Peyton," Helton yelled, "I can answer my own questions, thank you."

Manning was just so eager to prove he knew the answer, he couldn't help it. And if he didn't know the answer, he would ask.

"During the fall, I asked so many questions, coach Cutcliffe told me I'd give him an ulcer by the time I left here," Manning said. "My number one priority was to be a student of the game."

Said Cutcliffe: "A lot of bright people not only want to know what, but how and why. Peyton wants to understand. I appreciate that about Peyton. It's important enough to him that everything you say, he writes down. And he remembers what you said. That can come back to haunt you as a coach."

It haunted Cutcliffe. More than once he gave instructions about a play differently than he had a few weeks before. Manning would glance back in his notebook and correct his coach.

Tennessee's 1994 recruiting class was ranked number one by recruiting analysts. The main reasons: Manning and Stewart, two of the top 10 quarterbacks in the nation. Manning was the Gatorade Circle of Champions national player of the year. Stewart, the top quarterback in Texas, was considered a clone of former Tennessee great Heath Shuler, a strong-armed quarterback who provided a running threat. Thus, the first day of freshman practice drew greater media attention than usual. It was a day Manning would like to forget.

Manning threw the ball poorly. His passes were wobbly and off target. He overthrew; he underthrew. This guy was rated by some analysts the top quarterback in the nation? Stewart, meanwhile, threw with zip and accuracy. He fired spiral after spiral. He left no doubt who was ahead after the first duel.

"I didn't have a good first day," said Manning The reason? "New footballs," he said. "Peyton Manning and brand new footballs don't go well together. I was frustrated. I remember reading (in the newspaper) Branndon Stewart looked better than Peyton Manning. That bothered me."

From then on, Manning rubbed down the footballs before practice much like a pitcher rubs a baseball to get a better grip. It paid off. Manning began passing like Manning could. But he didn't look any better than Stewart.

Besides slick footballs, Manning was hit with another distraction. Despite his high grade-point average and satisfactory admissions' tests, Manning was incurring difficulty getting cleared by the NCAA Clearinghouse, a first-year organization that validated all curricula and test scores taken by student-athletes. Four times his test score was sent in; four times it apparently was lost.

At the time, freshmen had a 10-day grace period to practice. About half way through the grace period, in mid-August, recruiting coordinator Randy Sanders escorted Manning to a telephone after practice in an attempt to clear up the matter. Finally, before the 10 days were up,

Peyton laughs with long-time Tennessee senior associate athletic director Gus Manning (no relation). In the first meeting between the two, Peyton had been told that Gus was Knoxville Mayor Victor Ashe, leading to an embarrassing exchange.

Manning was cleared.

Meanwhile, Manning kept an inquisitive eye on his freshman competition.

"Peyton was looking at Branndon ... watching every move," Cutcliffe said.

At Tennessee's first full-scale scrimmage, Manning completed 10 of 12 passes. If you didn't know better, you would have thought he was Tennessee's starting quarterback. Maybe the Saints should have drafted him, rather than sign Jim Everett as a free agent. Of course, what did it really matter in August, 1994? Manning wouldn't play. He wouldn't make an impact. Unless ...

Colquitt's knee injury devastated Tennessee's coaching staff. After Colquitt went down, Cutcliffe said he panicked during the UCLA game. Colquitt, who grew up 30 miles from Tennessee's campus, was considered a budding star. He came close to beating out Shuler in the spring of 1992. Colquitt had the edge mentally. Shuler was more gifted physically.

When Tennessee coaches went with Shuler, Colquitt considered transferring. But he stuck it out, knowing he likely would get to start just one season. In preseason scrimmages, Colquitt was a sizzling 33 of 41 passes, including 10-for-10 in the last major scrimmage before the 1994 season. Then, it all went up in smoke on the first series of his senior season. Later that year, Colquitt's father died of a heart attack, adding to his woes.

Cutcliffe's heart went out to Colquitt. But he had to get his quarterbacks prepared for the rest of a challenging season. Tennessee's next game was at Georgia. Helton would start, with Manning and Stewart battling for the backup role. After the Vols arrived at UCLA, Fulmer had told Manning, "If you keep going at this rate, you could move past Todd." Manning got goose bumps.

Manning thought about that the week of the Georgia game.

Helton thought about something else. He knocked on the door during an offensive film session the Sunday after the UCLA game. He told Cutcliffe he had to see him, right now. Cutcliffe told Helton to wait. Helton wouldn't.

Cutcliffe went to his office with Helton and heard these encouraging words: "Coach, you know I'm a baseball player. I've tried, but I really haven't been paying attention. I really don't have any idea what to do. I can't go to Georgia and play quarterback."

Hello. Wasn't this the same cocky guy who told Cutcliffe during the fourth quarter of the UCLA game: "Coach, when you've got a bad pitcher on the mound, you've got to call a good game. So get off your butt and let's get going."

What happened to that guy?

Cutcliffe was stunned. He didn't dare tell the other offensive assistants. But he devised a game plan to limit Helton's role. Against Georgia, Tennessee ran the ball 71 times for 383 yards. The Vols won 41-23.

"Now you know why we only threw 13 times," Cutcliffe said. "I wasn't sure where they (passes) were going — and neither was Todd."

Manning sat on the bench the entire game. Never played a snap. It was the only time in his seven years of high school or college football that he didn't play in a game. The next week, Manning played sparingly in a 31-0 loss to Florida at Neyland Stadium. But he was robbed of one of the few shining moments in the game for Tennessee.

Manning threw what would have been his first touchdown pass late in the fourth quarter against the Gators, a 17-yard strike to Nilo Silvan. The score was nullified because Manning was beyond the line of scrimmage when he passed. Referee Jimmy Harper, an official when Archie Manning played at Ole Miss in the late 1960s, threw the flag. Harper was such a good friend of the family, he would send Archie a letter four years later, proclaiming the results of the Heisman Trophy race "a disgrace."

"Geez, Mr. Harper, please gimme a break," Peyton said.

"Sorry, Peyton, can't do it," Harper replied.

Harper remembers seeing Peyton trot onto the field that game.

"I had a funny feeling in my stomach," Harper said. "I felt old as hell because I was out there with the son of probably the greatest quarterback the SEC ever had."

Harper later recalled Peyton Manning was always polite to the officials.

"It was 'yes sir, no sir,' never a smart aleck type thing," Harper said." I never heard an official say anything about him except that he was gracious. I'm sure many times he'd liked to have said something to an official, but he never did."

While the Florida defeat was a downer, Manning was a short week away from a landmark moment. Tennessee played Mississippi State in Starkville, Miss., on Sept. 24. It would be Manning's only game during his college career on Mississippi soil, in the state where his father gained legendary status as an All-American quarterback at Ole Miss.

On third-and-30, Cutcliffe called a quarterback draw for Helton. If Cutcliffe had been a catcher and Helton the pitcher, Helton would have shaken off the pitch. But Cutcliffe was a coach. Helton ran the play. He gained 13 yards but he hurt his knee. Helton, miffed at the call, would be lost for the season. Suddenly, a Tennessee team that was 1-2, was down to two true freshman quarterbacks: Manning and Stewart. One or both would decide whether Tennessee would beat Mississippi State. The big picture was more bleak. How would Tennessee survive the season with a pair of rookies running the team?

Cutcliffe tried to rid his mind of such thoughts. There was a game to be won. Perhaps forgetting he didn't have Colquitt at the controls, Cutcliffe called a deep out route. Manning never threw it in high school. The deep out is a college or pro route. It takes a rifle arm to complete. It defines whether you have the strength to play in the NFL.

Manning was confident.

"I was pretty good at throwing that route," he said later.

The primary receiver was Kendrick Jones. He was guarded by Bulldogs cornerback Charlie Davidson, a track sprinter. Jones ran a deep out. Manning threw across the field. Davidson broke on the ball. Davidson smelled an interception. He was going against some rookie quarterback. He'd show the kid not to throw in his direction.

As Davidson reached up for the ball, a funny thing happened. The ball wasn't there. It was in Jones's hands. Davidson learned something about the youngster; he had an arm.

Jones turned up the sideline and sprinted 76 yards for a touchdown. Manning stood in the spot where he delivered the ball, in shock. He looked to the sideline and saw two freshman colleagues - Cory Gaines and Terry Fair - cheering for him.

Guard Bubba Miller quickly gave Manning some advice. After a touchdown pass, pat your linemen on the behind and go down field to congratulate your receiver. Manning would follow that advice 88 more times in his college career.

Manning completed 14 of 23 passes for 256 yards and two touchdowns in his coming-out party. Archie's boy was brilliant in his first college game in the state of Mississippi. But not all went well. The day would have a sour ending. Tennessee had five turnovers on its last five possessions and lost to the underdog Bulldogs.

Stewart threw a key interception that curbed UT's momentum. Manning threw an interception, and, in the UT section of orange, a lone person stood and cheered - Vickie Stewart, Branndon's mother.

This quarterback controversy was about to get ugly.

Branndon's parents, enraged at what they perceived to be mistreatment of their son, drove from Starkville to Knoxville to visit with Fulmer and Cutcliffe on Sunday. No solution was reached.

"The Stewarts as parents were looking at two freshman who had both been here an equal amount of time," Cutcliffe said. "They wondered why one (Manning) would come in first all the time. It was hurting their son's confidence. They said, 'If you let him (Branndon) go in first some, he'd have a chance to prove himself.' I understood that."

The Stewarts were bothered by the possibility that Manning, being the son of a famous SEC quarterback, was getting preferential treatment.

"Truth be known, Peyton was much more prepared to play," Cutcliffe said. "Branndon was a good football player, but we were probably more unfair to Peyton. Peyton was more prepared to play. Peyton knew that. Jerry Colquitt knew that. Todd Helton knew that. Sure, Branndon knew that, too. He didn't know half of what Peyton knew. Peyton outworked Branndon.

"But Branndon's mother knew more about coaching than I did."

The competition drove a wedge between the two quarterbacks. For a while, they hardly spoke to one another outside of football.

"It was never a problem between he and I," Peyton Manning said four years later. "He and I were always friends. I wish he'd played another position because I think he and I would have been best friends."

Indeed, two years later, Manning was in a hurry to get off the practice field in late August. He wanted to watch Texas A&M play Brigham Young in the Pigskin Classic. Why? The Aggies were quarterbacked by a former teammate, Branndon Stewart.

With turmoil at quarterback, Tennessee began the '94 season 1-3.

"I was thinking, 'Tennessee is supposed to be better than this,'" Manning said.

The Vols had a serious quarterback dilemma. It wouldn't go away, partly because Tennessee coaches wouldn't step up and declare Manning the starter for fear of offending Stewart. Manning had played extremely well against Mississippi State. Stewart had not. Yet, Fulmer wouldn't give the job to Manning, at least, not publicly.

In the offensive meeting room, a chair in the front row is reserved for Tennessee's starting quarterback. The week of the Washington State game, nobody sat there. Not Manning. Not Stewart. Nobody. It was left empty.

"Peyton stared a hole in that seat," Cutcliffe said. "That was an issue with Peyton."

Offensive practices were sloppy that week. Three receivers were hurt. The passing game was out of sync. It was so bad on Thursday, Cutcliffe decided to scale back the offense and rely on the defense to beat Washington State. The Cougars had the nation's top-ranked defense but a terrible offense. Cutcliffe didn't want Washington State's defense to set up any easy points. Friday before the game, as expected, Fulmer named Manning the starter.

"I got the seat," Manning said proudly, "and never gave it up."

"There was no way anybody was going to get him out of that seat, nor should anybody else even bother to sit in it," Cutcliffe said.

Tennessee had two offensive plays that gained over 20 yards against Washington State, and won a boring contest, 10-9. On his very first series, Manning threw an interception that the officials ruled incomplete. Had the officials not blown the call and the Cougars won, no telling how Tennessee's season and Manning's career would have evolved.

"Thank the Lord they didn't call that an interception," Manning said.

The victory would turn Tennessee's season around, but it wouldn't stem the quarterback debate. Manning had completed just 7-of-14 for 79 yards against the Cougars. Tennessee was 3-3 and unranked entering the Alabama game. The Crimson Tide, which hadn't lost to the Vols since 1985, was 6-0 and ranked.

Tennessee trailed 17-13 in the finals minutes when Manning drove the Vols inside the Alabama 10. On fourth down, Manning threw an incomplete pass to the left side to Silvan. To the right, running back James Stewart was wide open. He would easily have picked up a first down, if not scored.

After the game, Fulmer said Manning threw to the wrong side.

"I did not throw to the wrong side and I'll argue with anyone who says I did," said Manning, issuing a direct rebuttal to his head coach.

It was a gutsy thing to say. Here's a young guy fighting for the quarterback job and he's taking on his coach in public. He had done what he was coached to do, and, by God, he wasn't going to take criticism for that.

Against a blitz from both sides, Manning was taught to throw in the direction where he had the most pass blockers. Against Alabama, that was to the left side. That rule applies only if the quarterback is under center; Manning was in the shotgun. But Cutcliffe had not explained that to Manning.

"As a coach, I let him down," Cutcliffe said. "I went straight to the locker room and hugged his neck. He had tears in his eyes. I told him how proud I was of him as a player, that he did exactly what he was coached to do. ... He didn't deserve any criticism of missing an open receiver. He did not miss an open receiver."

Surely, Fulmer meant no malice. He was simply pointing out that Manning didn't see an open receiver. But after Manning read what Fulmer said in the paper, Manning went to his coach.

"Coach, I didn't throw to the wrong side, and I didn't appreciate reading where you were second guessing me in the paper," Manning said. Fulmer said, "Well, I made a mistake. It won't happen again."

It's easy for a freshman, or even a veteran, to be intimidated by the head coach. But Manning felt if he couldn't say what was on his mind to Fulmer, then they didn't have the right kind of relationship.

Other fireworks exploded after the game.

Stewart had played just one series. He was upset. His parents were upset. His high school coach, Art Briles of Stephenville, Texas, was upset. Manning had not played that well against Alabama: 10-of-18 for 138 yards and two interceptions. Stewart, many felt, deserved to play more, considering he guided the Vols to a field goal late in the first half. ESPN announcers speculated Stewart would start the second half. Instead, he didn't take another snap.

Fulmer's explanation: "He ran 13 plays and had five busts."

"And three points," Briles countered.

After the game, Vicky Stewart beat on the UT locker room door, screaming to be admitted. After all, she just knew Archie Manning was in there, too. She just knew Tennessee's coaches were catering to Peyton's father.

"I was not in the locker room," Archie Manning said.

Interestingly, Cutcliffe said the way Manning brought Tennessee to the brink of victory against Alabama, "Laid the foundation of being a man when it comes to being a quarterback in the SEC."

When it came to that last drive against Alabama, "Peyton's instincts took over," Cutcliffe said.

"I wanted to be in the game," Manning said. "I wasn't going to say, 'Put Branndon in, he's playing well right now, we have a better chance to win with him.' I was going to say, 'No, I want to be in there.'"

The Manning-Stewart controversy assumed a life of its own. It was the hot topic in bars and barber shops. Fans, if not players, began to take sides. Yet, Fulmer refused to name a starter, even though everyone knew it was Manning. Fulmer was going overboard to keep Stewart appeased. The quarterbacks shared practice time, with Manning playing the majority on game day.

Two games later, the controversy reared its head again.

Manning had the worst game of his Tennessee career against Memphis. He was 5-of-12 for 32 yards. It looked like he was passing with those dreaded new footballs. As he struggled, he also got booed. Booed like his father was booed at Saints games. Booed like NFL guys get booed for bad performances. But this was college. And this was a college freshman, for crying out loud. This was supposed to be different, wasn't it?

Not really.

"I wasn't aware there were that many boos in college football, especially on a day when you're winning," Peyton said.

Fans were booing Manning in favor of Stewart.

"That's when I realized this is a Branndon-Peyton thing," Manning said. "It's not really all for Tennessee."

Cutcliffe chastised the fans for booing college players.

"If they (quarterbacks) are getting booed, they ought to feel like the fans are booing me because I'm the one who ought to have them ready," Cutcliffe said.

Stewart didn't help his cause because he didn't play well, either. But, somehow, Tennessee managed to win. The battle lines became closer between Manning and Stewart. And speculation grew: Would Manning start the next week against Kentucky?

Manning said later he's not sure if the quarterback situation created a divisive force within the team.

"I was not campaigning for myself," he said. "Whether the linemen or wide receivers had favorites, who knows."

But Manning did know two things: First, he wasn't going to play that poorly again, and second, if he hadn't started the next week against Kentucky, "Coach Fulmer would have heard from me again because we won."

Manning started the next week, and Tennessee got on a roll. The Vols beat Kentucky 52-0, routed Vanderbilt 65-0 in Gerry DiNardo's last game as Commodores' coach, and ripped Virginia Tech 45-23 in the

Gator Bowl. They scored 162 points in three games, an average of 54 points per game.

Down the stretch, Manning not only proved he had control of the offense, he showed some running skills that no one thought existed. He looked too slow, too awkward to escape a rush and gain yards. But against Kentucky, he scored on a 10-yard run. And against Virginia Tech, he broke past the line of scrimmage, faked a defender and rambled 32 yards.

"I can run, too," Manning proclaimed.

Kentucky players said their team speed was woefully inadequate if Manning could run for a touchdown. Manning didn't take too kindly to that remark.

"I was sort of sensitive at that time," Manning said of his speed, which he increased in the 40-yard dash from about 4.95 seconds in high school to 4.82 as a senior.

The run against the Hokies might have run Stewart out of town. Stewart had said two weeks before the bowl game he was returning to Tennessee and looking forward to a spring practice challenge with Manning. But two weeks after the bowl game, Stewart returned to campus, packed his bags and transferred to Texas A&M.

As Manning's career at Tennessee was unfolding, Stewart's folded. Pressured by his parents to leave, Stewart told them in early January during a ski trip he would abide by their wishes. The rumor which had surfaced three months earlier that he was going to Texas A&M came true. Vicky Stewart said the family had invested too much money in Branndon for him to sit on the bench behind Manning throughout college and ruin a pro career.

"I thought the bowl game was an opportunity to close the deal," Manning said. "I was thinking, 'No way we could do this again next year.' The bowl game had a little more to it besides winning. I wanted to shine. I wanted to be the starting quarterback at Tennessee full time, not every third series."

Said Cutcliffe: "Not to be ugly, but Branndon Stewart was probably convinced that (Manning) was a great quarterback playing, and against a real quality defensive football team, Peyton put on a show.

"Branndon Stewart was an awfully good player, but there was still a difference."

Manning was named the SEC Freshman of the Year by *The Knoxville News-Sentinel*. He had one of the top 15 statistical seasons ever for a true freshman in Division 1-A.

That left him thirsty for other goals.

"I wanted to be the REAL All-SEC quarterback, even All-American," Manning said. "But what I was most proud of was being 7-1 as a starter."

And sitting in the chair to the front row of the staff meeting room. The one reserved for Tennessee's starting quarterback.

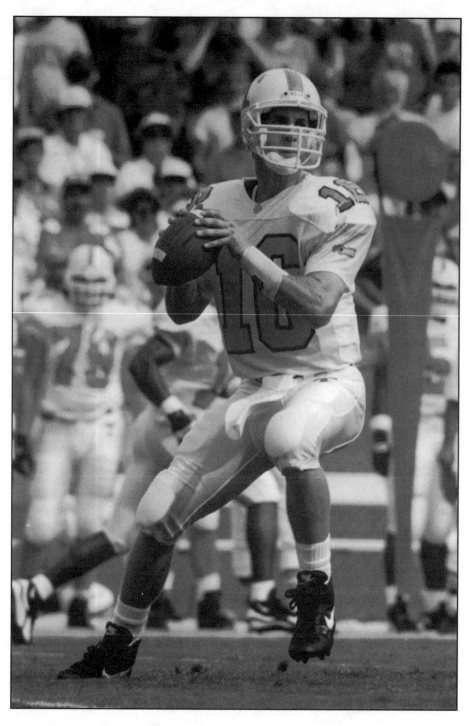

Despite an impressive freshman season, Manning saw the need to quicken his delivery by holding the ball higher. It was one of many examples of Manning's eagerness to improve.

Chapter Five:

The Playmaker

"Good God, what a play! What a player!"

– David Cutcliffe
Tennessee offensive coordinator

YOU'VE COMPLETED 61.8 PERCENT OF YOUR PASSES AS a true freshman in Division 1-A. You threw 11 touchdown passes and had only six interceptions. You passed for 7,207 yards and 92 touchdowns in high school. Your dad was an All-American and All-Pro quarterback.

You *know* how to throw the football.

Yet, entering your sophomore year at Tennessee, you tinker with your passing mechanics. Are you crazy? Or just possessed to be a success?

One overwhelming trait about Peyton Manning is his uncanny determination to improve. If he completes 20 of 22 passes, he anguishes about the two incompletions. "He never wanted to stop getting better," Cutcliffe said.

At the beginning of his sophomore year, Peyton Manning thought a change was needed for two reasons. One, to give him a quicker release, and, two, to make him more accurate - as if 61.8 percent wasn't accurate enough.

Manning raised the ball higher in his release. Rather than begin his throwing motion from the chest area, he held the ball closer to his right ear.

"My freshman year, I found myself bringing the ball lower," Manning said. "The motion was good. It was just taking longer to get rid of the ball. So I figured with guys blitzing and coming at you, I needed a quicker release."

It wasn't an easy transition. It wasn't like going from a slice to a fade. It was like going to a cross-handed putting style.

"It was a difficult task for a quarterback," Cutcliffe said. "You've been holding the ball the same way for years, and the ball feels comfortable in your hand. Now you're changing the way the ball fits into your fingers."

And remember, there were no guarantees it would improve Manning's accuracy - only his release time.

"It was an intense period of time for us to work through that so he could be as effective and as accurate and as comfortable with it as possible," Cutcliffe said.

Quick results were necessary because the Vols opened the 1995 season against dangerous East Carolina, talented Georgia and two-time defending SEC champion Florida.

Manning completed 17 of 29 passes against East Carolina, but the litmus test was Georgia the next week. Before a national ESPN audience, Manning was brilliant. He hit 26 of 38 passes. He torched the Bulldogs for 349 yards and two touchdowns. Some called it the best game they'd ever seen played by a Tennessee quarterback.

"My coming-out party," Manning said of Tennessee's 30-27 victory at Neyland Stadium.

He made the right reads. Made the right throws. He even marched the team down the field for a game-winning field goal in the final seconds after an ill-advised, throw-across-the-body interception in Tennessee territory almost led to an upset loss.

"I felt like I really helped the team win, whereas other times, I just did my part and tried not to get the team beat," Manning said.

A star was born. Two stars, really.

That night it became evident that the rest of the SEC would have to deal with Manning-to-Joey Kent for two more years. Kent caught 69 passes in 1995 and 68 in 1996. He could become Tennessee's all-time leading receiver with 183 catches.

In 1994, when Manning was a freshman, Cutcliffe asked the young quarterback which receivers looked impressive.

"This guy Joey Kent can run and get the ball," Manning said.

Kent did just that against Georgia in 1995. In the third quarter, Kent, rendered silent most of the first half, told Manning in his soft-spoken voice: "Get me involved."

"That's all he said," said Manning. "He didn't complain. He didn't say, 'You're not throwing to me.' He said, 'Just get me the ball.'"

On that drive, Manning hit Kent on three consecutive passes, the latter one for a touchdown. "Is that involved enough for you?" Manning asked Kent.

It was the beginning of a lethal combination.

"He didn't say much to me, I didn't say much to him," Manning said. "We just sort of had a feel for one another. Sometimes, he'd run the wrong route but it's like I expected him to run the wrong route."

The next game, however, would be a source of great frustration for Manning and the Vols. Tennessee led Florida 30-14 late in the first half. Manning was clicking on short and long throws.

"We felt we might blow them out; this game should be ours," Manning said.

It wasn't. In the final seconds of the first half, Florida scored to make it 30-21. Tennessee took the second-half kickoff, marched inside the 10 but missed a field goal. Then, Jay Graham fumbled on consecutive possessions.

It was about to rain on Tennessee's parade - literally. Florida scored 48 unanswered points for a 62-37 victory and a downpour saturated the Vols' uniforms and hopes in the waning minutes.

"It's hard to even talk about the way it turned out," Manning said, three years later.

It would actually be Tennessee's best chance to beat Florida in Manning's four years. In 1996, the Vols trailed 35-0 and in 1997, Florida jumped to a 14-0 lead.

A month later, Manning played perhaps his best game in a Tennessee

Peyton often found reason to celebrate with receiver Joey Kent in the end zone. Kent caught 137 passes his last two seasons combined and became the school's all-time leading receiver.

uniform. It was homecoming at Arkansas. The Vols took that as an insult. Weren't homecoming opponents supposed to be patsies?

Arkansas' defensive coordinator was Joe Lee Dunn, known for his unconventional defenses. When he was at Ole Miss, he once lined up without any defensive linemen, then went to a 2-4-5 (two down linemen, four linebackers and five defensive backs). He liked to pressure quarterbacks and disguise defenses.

Dunn hoped to confuse this upstart quarterback at Tennessee into making a myriad of mistakes.

"Joe Lee Dunn is going to bring the safety, the cornerback, every single linebacker," Manning said. "You don't know where they're coming from. This was my first real test as a starting quarterback. Can he handle the pressure? Can he handle the blitz?"

The answers: How about 35 completions in 46 attempts for 384 yards and four touchdowns? How about 49 points against what was the SEC's top-ranked defense? How about an 18-point victory against a team that would eventually win the West Division and play in the SEC Championship game?

Final score: Tennessee 49, Arkansas 31.

Manning checked off on almost every play. He walked from tackle to tackle, telling guys who to block. He turned his back to the defense and screamed at his backs to make sure they knew the new play. He pointed to receivers, making sure they caught the audible.

Then he orchestrated play after successful play. Manning had outfoxed the fox.

"A lot of times, playing quarterback is easy," Manning said. "You drop back and throw.

"Well, when you work hard before the play within the 25-second clock and you get something done, it's a good feeling. ... That was a special day for me. Playing a game within a game, those are the fun things for me."

It wasn't so fun in the second half when Arkansas linebacker Anthony Hicks blitzed through and rocked Manning from behind well after Manning had thrown the football.

Peyton pointed Tennessee to a high-scoring victory over eventual SEC West Division champion Arkansas in 1995. Manning was brilliant in his first real test against a pressure, blitzing defense as a starting quarterback.

"They're a blitzing team," Cutcliffe said. "That's they're focus. So the intimidation of the quarterback is the whole deal. Peyton had his back to a defender and the guy comes over there and tries to flatten him, tries to knock his head off."

This came from the same Arkansas team whose coach, Danny Ford, was heard by a television camera yelling "I hope he tears up a knee," at Tennessee quarterback Heath Shuler in the finals minutes of a game in 1993.

"I'm not taking that," said Manning, who got in Hicks' face and exchanged a few words. "I gave him a little lip service and let him know I didn't like it one bit."

The quarterback who a year ago had been told to shut the bleep up in the huddle by one of his own offensive lineman, found those same lineman coming to his defense. He had earned their respect.

"Arkansas got on the wrong side of Peyton Manning," Cutcliffe said.

The next week, Manning faced another major test. Tennessee hadn't beaten hated-rival Alabama since 1985. The losses were excruciating. In 1986, Alabama scored 56 points. In 1987, the Tide humiliated Tennessee 41-22 on ESPN. Tennessee's only loss in 1989 was to Alabama. In 1990, a blocked field-goal attempt led to a game-winning field goal for Alabama. In 1993, Tennessee had control of the game until the Tide scored in the final seconds and made a two-point conversion to tie.

Nine years. Eight losses. One tie. One angry group of fans.

"When I first got to Tennessee, fans said, 'Peyton, just beat Alabama for us. We don't care if we go 1-10 as long as you beat Alabama,'" Manning said.

Tennessee was 5-1 and confident entering the Alabama game.

"We felt like we were a better team," Manning said. "We weren't going to let a final play or a blocked kick or a tipped pass stop us. We're gonna beat 'em and we've got a chance to beat 'em badly."

Cutcliffe is a Birmingham native who signed to play football at Alabama. He had grown tired of losing to the Tide. In the locker room before the game, he told Manning the Vols might open up with a pass.

Manning's bootleg against Alabama was his signature play as Tennessee snapped a nine-year winless streak against a heated rival in 1995.

Cutcliffe has been known to change his mind, so Manning didn't hold his breath.

This time, Cutcliffe didn't change his mind. On Tennessee's first play, Manning hit Kent on a quick slant over the middle. Kent caught the ball, cut left, then outraced the defense to the end zone for an electrifying 80- yard touchdown.

One play. One touchdown. One jinx snapped.

"After that, you knew the game was over," Manning said of Tennessee's 41-14 victory. "It was a party the whole night."

The early touchdown pass wasn't Manning's signature play in the game, however. His signature play came later. The Vols led comfortably and were on the Alabama 1-yard line. "Power right, two power" was the play sent in from the bench. Assistant coach Randy Sanders, who signals in the plays, pointed to Manning.

Uh, oh. That meant a fake. Manning would pretend to hand off to Graham diving over the middle, and bootleg to the left.

Manning told no one, not even Graham.

Manning bobbled the snap — "If I'd fumbled the snap, I'd have never lived it down" — and faked giving the ball to Graham. Eleven Alabama players converged on Graham. Tennessee lineman Jason Layman, not knowing Graham didn't have the ball, looked at the back leaping over the pile and raised both hands to signal "touchdown." An official, looking at Graham, signaled touchdown.

And there's Manning, not an Alabama player within 15 yards, practically waltzing into the end zone for a touchdown.

"That was a shining moment for me," Manning said.

After the game, Manning puffed on the customary victory cigar along with his teammates. You could hardly breathe in the Tennessee locker room. Nine years of bondage had been lifted. Manning was elated.

"I realized what we'd done," Manning said. "It was more than just a win on Saturday night. It meant a lot."

It meant so much, Manning got angry with Cutcliffe. With the game in hand, Cutcliffe throttled down the offense, not wanting to run up the score.

After one series, Manning made a bee-line to the headphones to talk to Cutcliffe, who was in the press box.

"What's up? What are you doing?" screamed Manning.

"Peyton, Peyton, Peyton," Cutcliffe said. "Don't worry. Let's get the game over and enjoy it."

Manning didn't get to enjoy it as much as he wanted. He wasn't able to join his teammates for the post-game celebration on the field. ESPN sideline reporter Mike Adamle held up Manning for an interview. Manning was ansty, glaring at the end-zone scene.

"I'm depriving this man of his once in a lifetime opportunity here," Adamle said. The disgusted look on Manning's face didn't go away.

Peyton had to run off brother Cooper before talking to Cutcliffe via the press box telephone. Cooper heckled Peyton after he threw a first-quarter interception against Kentucky in 1995.

"Everybody was over there going crazy and I didn't get to get any of it," Manning said. "It bothered me."

Three games later, Tennessee's hope for a one-loss season was in the balance at Kentucky, in a game dubbed the Battle for the Beer Barrel. It was a cold day at Commonwealth Stadium.

Cooper Manning, then a senior at Ole Miss, was trying to break into broadcasting. Bob Kesling, sports director of WBIR Channel 10 in Knoxville and a member of the Jefferson-Pilot SEC game of the week crew, got a media pass for Cooper to be the sideline reporter and keep track of Tennessee's injuries.

Early in the game, Peyton threw an interception. As Peyton went to the sideline phone to talk to Cutcliffe in the press box, Cooper went to Peyton and started chewing him out.

"What kind of play was that?" Cooper screamed. "What were you thinking?"

Peyton, surprised to see his brother on the sideline, wasn't amused.

"What are you doing here?" Peyton said. "Get out of here. I'll call security and have you thrown out of here!"

Peyton recovered and rallied the Vols to a 34-31 victory, passing for 272 yards and two touchdowns.

Tennessee finished the regular-season 10-1. Manning set school records by completing 244 of 380 passes for 2,964 yards and 22 touchdowns. He threw just four interceptions.

Tennessee lost the SEC's East Division to Florida, and got snubbed by the first-year Bowl Coalition because it was required to invite Notre Dame if the Irish had eight wins. Notre Dame went to the Fiesta Bowl.

Tennessee, tied for fourth in the nation with Ohio State, went to the Florida Citrus Bowl to play the Buckeyes, who had lost their chance of winning a national title with yet another November defeat to Michigan.

Tennessee took the game seriously, but the players enjoyed their second trip in three years to Orlando.

Manning had his picture taken with Bullwinkle The Moose at Universal Studios. Given Peyton's long neck, his teammates thought they saw

Manning passed Tennessee to a 20-14 victory over No. 4 Ohio State in the 1996 Citrus bowl. The Buckeyes were the highest-ranked team Manning defeated during his Tennessee career.

quite a resemblance between Manning and the moose. They called Manning Bullwinkle the rest of the night.

Manning was in rare form, offering to impersonate his receivers.

"You want to hear my impersonation of Peerless Price: Were you open Peerless?

"Oh, man, you know I was open.

"Want to hear my impersonation of Marcus Nash: Were you open, Marcus?

"Uh, huh; uh, huh; uh, huh.

"Want to hear my impersonation of Dustin Moore: Were you open Dustin?

"Was I supposed to go out on that play?"

Ohio State was the most talented team Tennessee played that year, and one of the most talented teams Manning played against in college. They had a Heisman Trophy winner in Eddie George, the Outland and Lombardi winner in tackle Orlando Pace, a great receiver in Terry Glenn, and a dozen other players who eventually would be drafted in the NFL.

Graham ran 69 yards for a touchdown late in the first half to propel the Vols to a 20-14 victory on a rainy day.

"That game against Ohio State was a huge win for our program, for Coach Fulmer, and for me personally because we beat a great team, a team that could have been national champions that year," Manning said.

"Sure, you want to be No. 1, you want to go undefeated. But to finish No. 2 in the country (in the coaches' poll) ahead of Florida, who had beaten us earlier in the season, we felt we'd done something special that year."

The game was not without controversy. Ohio State coach John Cooper, a native of Knoxville, complained after the game that Tennessee used illegal cleats to help with footing on the damp field. Cooper had an aide actually finagle his way into the Tennessee locker room after the game and steal a shoe to prove his case.

Cooper said he pleaded with officials before the game to check Tennessee's cleats. The officials refused, Cooper said. An Ohio State assistant, Lovie Smith, was on Tennessee's staff for the 1994 Citrus Bowl when the Vols allegedly used long cleats in a 35-10 loss to Penn State. Smith, now playing against the Vols, had warned Cooper about Tennessee's tactics.

Tennessee admitted 19 players used cleats that were to long, but blamed it on a mix-up with a shoe company from Cookeville, Tenn., that sent the team soccer cleats, rather than football cleats.

Tennessee could have helped its case by revealing the names of the 19 players. If they were all backs and receivers, then suspicions would grow. If some linemen were in the mix, then Tennessee could argue it was happenstance. Tennessee refused to reveal the names of the players who wore the elongated cleats.

The next year, the NCAA rules committee implemented what was known as the "Tennessee Rule," which said that any player wearing an illegal cleat - knowingly or not - would be suspended for the next game.

Long cleats weren't the worst of Tennessee's woes. Expectations were. The win over Ohio State had preseason prognosticators picking the Vols to win the national championship. The Vols had lost the bulk of a strong offensive line, but so did Nebraska after the 1994 season and the Cornhuskers repeated. Surely Manning, Nash and Graham could overcome a weakened line.

"No. 1 in the country sounds so good, but it's so much better after the season," said Manning, sounding a warning signal for his team. "Coach Fulmer told us early, don't believe the hype.

"Well, it's hard not to get caught up in that. We had a lot of players who believed it. You want to have confidence, but you want to be humble going in and say you'll earn your way there.

"I don't know if we were overconfident, but we believed the No. 1 ranking and got caught up in that. It ended up hurting us."

Tennessee almost lost its second game of the season, to UCLA, whose offensive line coach, Steve Marshall, worked at Tennessee the previous three years. An 86-yard punt return in the fourth quarter by Terry Fair gave the Vols a 28-13 lead. But an 88-yard touchdown pass by UCLA closed the margin to 28-20.

"I'm thinking, there's no way we can lose this game," Manning said. "If you have to do something different, take it into your own hands."

He did. On Tennessee's next possession, Manning told Kent if he audibled, run a hitch-and-go route. It was third-and-2. UCLA showed an eight-man front. A run play was called. Manning checked to a pass. But he forgot what he had told Kent. He forgot Kent was supposed to run a hitch-and-go. The ball was about to be snapped ... then he remembered.

Manning pumped faked to Kent on a quick out. UCLA's cornerback bit. Kent turned up field. Manning lofted a perfect strike.

"Our guys on the sideline said they could hear the cornerback say, 'Oh, God,'" Manning said.

Kent caught the pass. He had a 53-yard touchdown. He had the game won. Tennessee, preseason No. 1 Tennessee, had escaped a major upset.

"It's one of those plays where if you're a veteran, you can change something like that and get away with it - as long as it works," Manning said.

The next game was Florida. Most everyone gave Tennessee a chance to beat the Gators in Neyland Stadium. In the spring, in the summer, during two-a-day practices in August, Tennessee periodically worked on a scheme that would beat Florida's passing attack. The Vols opened with a nickel package, moving safety Tori Noel to left outside linebacker, behind end Leonard Little, and inserting another safety into the lineup.

Spurrier must have known something. He came out running at Little and Noel. Florida scored on its first drive, completing a fourth-and-11 pass from the 35 when a safety got out of position.

Florida went up 35-0 after 20 minutes. Manning had a poor first half, throwing four interceptions, two of which came off tipped passes. He rallied in the second half to cut Florida's lead to 35-29, but it was too little, too late. Manning finished with a career-high 492 passing yards and four touchdowns.

After the game, CBS color analyst Craig James accused Manning of having "happy feet" in the pocket. That infuriated Cutcliffe.

Peyton Manning: Primed and Ready

"Craig James obviously doesn't know as much about quarterbacks as I thought he did," Cutcliffe said. "It's a very poor evaluation of a player. He doesn't understand what happy feet are.

"As far as I'm concerned, Craig James couldn't coach a quarterback at a junior high school. He hasn't got a clue."

Had James done his homework, he would have known that Tennessee teaches its quarterbacks to pat their feet in the pocket. The idea is to give them better balance in changing the direction of a pass. The longer the quarterback holds the ball, the more he taps his feet, and the more it appears he's getting nervous in the pocket.

Manning took his happy feet to Memphis for Tennessee's next game. It was the game everybody in the Manning family felt uneasy about, Peyton included. It was the game against Ole Miss, Archie's alma mater. In 1986, Archie Manning became the first - and only - Rebel football player to have his number retired. No one in Ole Miss sports history is more revered than Archie Manning.

The game would be played on Oct. 3, on ESPN.

Archie Manning knew he would be in demand before the game.

"You're getting an exclusive because I don't plan to do many of these things," Archie said of interviews about his son playing against his alma mater. Archie and Olivia ducked out of sight, traveling to Destin, Fla., the week before the game, seeking seclusion. But before they left, Archie Manning talked about what a difficult 12 days it would be for him.

"I'd just as soon not deal with it," Archie said. "I just don't plan to get in the middle of it. I know a lot of people want opinions on this or that. I don't plan to do that 100 times."

Archie feared the ill-feelings that surfaced after Peyton committed to Tennessee would resurface.

It would be difficult for Peyton, too. Peyton listened to all those Ole Miss football tapes when his dad played quarterback. He memorized the starting lineups from those 1968-70 teams. He had assumed most of his life he would play for Ole Miss.

Now, he was wearing orange and white, playing against the team in red and blue.

"I knew I was going to have mixed emotions," Peyton said. "Sure enough, during warm-ups, I heard the Ole Miss band playing Hoddy Toddy and Dixie, and I saw those Ole Miss colors on the opposite side of the field. It was a difficult feeling for me."

But Peyton made one thing clear: "Rocky Top is my song."

Still, it was a strange situation. Strange because it was the son of an Ole Miss legend playing against Ole Miss. It was a story that not only captivated the South, but the nation.

Archie told Peyton: "You go play the game and let us handle this."

Said Peyton: "I know he was nervous that day. I know he wanted me to play well. I know he wanted Tennessee to win the ballgame because he was pulling for me.

"People were asking him who he was going for. Well, it was a no-brainer. He was going to pull for his son. But I know it was a tough week for him."

Peyton was extraordinarily intense in practices leading up to the Ole Miss game.

"I sure didn't want to go down there in front of a lot of people watching me and just flop and play badly and lose because I knew I'd never hear the end of it," Peyton said.

Archie sat in the sky box of the accounting firm of Morgan Keegan, which paid Ole Miss $1 million to move the game from Oxford to Memphis. He sat with noted author John Grisham, who named a judge in his book "The Client" after Archie Manning.

Bradley "Butch" Farris, the Newman assistant with strong Ole Miss ties, watched the game on ESPN.

"I wanted Peyton to throw for 400 yards and Ole Miss to win by one," Farris said.

Peyton put on a show. He completed 18 of 22 passes for 242 yards and one touchdown as the Vols prevailed 41-3. A game that was close at halftime turned into a rout.

"I'm glad all that's over with," Peyton said. "My dad can sleep the rest of the year."

If Archie was in a slumber, he was awakened by the next game. Manning exploded with a 371-yard performance against Georgia. He completed 31 of 41 passes as the Vols won in Athens 29-17.

"That game I can watch over and over and over again, and have fun and laugh," Manning said. "I think it was the best game I played just because things were clicking and I was making plays quarterbacks aren't supposed to make."

On one play, Manning stepped on his fullback's foot and tripped as he was dropping back, then, while falling down, flipped a completion to Jeremaine Copeland.

Then came THE PLAY.

Tennessee was on the Georgia 5-yard line, facing fourth-and-inches. Cutcliffe called a quarterback sneak. As the Vols went to the line, Georgia stationed two 320-pound tackles over center Brent Gibson.

"Brent said, 'There's no way in the world we're going to make it,'" Peyton said. "He was saying, 'Oh, God.'"

"As a quarterback, that's not what I want to hear."

With Gibson muttering "uh, oh," Manning took the snap. He churned his feet. He went nowhere. He stood up. Hearing no whistle, Manning began to give ground and roll to his right. He retreated to his 23-yard line.

If Cutcliffe had a gun, Manning might have been buried that night at Sanford Stadium. Here was a simple sneak, and Manning was running around with the ball on the 23.

As Manning approached the sideline, he glanced to make sure no linemen were downfield, then he fired into the end zone. Marcus Nash made a circus catch before falling out of bounds.

Touchdown Tennessee.

As Manning went to the sideline, he told the coaches, "Great call."

Fulmer's first comment: "What in the hell am I supposed to tell the media?"

Peyton: "Tell them it was a called play."

The play was nominated for an ESPY as one of college football's most bizarre moments in 1996.

"It's a play you laugh at," Manning said. "You can't do anything else but laugh. It'll never happen again in my career."

Cutcliffe described the play as indescribable. "When you grade film on Sunday, you sit there and think, 'Good God what a play! What a player!'" Cutcliffe said.

The next game, the euphoria of the Georgia victory was buried under the sea of a 13-0 Alabama third-quarter lead. The Vols rallied to tie the game in the fourth quarter.

With less than four minutes left, Cutcliffe called a play to run Graham off right tackle. Graham was smothered. Cutcliffe called the same play again.

"We're kind of playing for overtime, playing not to lose," Manning said.

Graham took the handoff, cut inside a block by Spencer Riley and raced 79 yards for a game-winning touchdown. Cutcliffe tells you he thought Graham had a chance to break it. Manning agrees, then snickers: "He's my coach."

Manning put Tennessee's second consecutive win over Alabama in perspective.

"In '95, we beat them badly," he said. "In '96, we beat them the way they'd beaten us for the past nine years. They were leading the game and we came back. An 80-yard run (actually 79) with a couple of minutes left is not supposed to happen. They knew that and we knew that."

Still, it didn't damper the post-game celebration. Vol players and coaches sang, some in tune:

"We don't give a damn about the whole state of Alabama, the whole state of Alabama, the whole state of Alabama;

"We don't give a damn about the whole state of Alabama, we're from Tennessee."

All this Manning Mania had Tennessee fans euphoric. After one home game, Tennessee fans spotted who they thought was Eli Manning, Peyton's younger brother and a sophomore quarterback at Newman

Tennessee closed out a 10-2 season with a resounding 48-28 victory over Northwestern in the 1997 Citrus Bowl. But the game is best remembered for Tennessee fans chanting ``one more year, one more year," to Manning.

High School. Instead, it was older brother Cooper Manning. But Cooper didn't correct the inquisitive Vol fans. Cooper signed Eli's name on a hat and wrote "Vol bound."

Another Tennessee fan walked by: "Eli, you gonna be a Vol?"

Cooper posing as Eli: "How much money you got?"

Fan: "I got plenty."

Archie, posing as a concerned parent with no intention of being introduced to an NCAA investigator, said: "Cooper, that's enough. You'll get us all in trouble."

The Vols were 6-1 going into the Memphis game. Win, and they play in a Bowl Alliance game. The unthinkable happened, however. In arguably the biggest upset in Tennessee history, the Vols lost to Memphis for the first time in 16 meetings, 21-17. Peyton Manning played poorly, throwing two interceptions. It was one of Manning's worst losses at Tennessee.

The next week, Manning got hurt against Arkansas on a tackle by Melvin Bradley. Manning suffered a strained medial collateral ligament in his right knee.

"I'm thinking, 'Maybe it is time to leave (turn pro) for sure,'" Manning said.

The next week, Tennessee reshuffled its offensive line. Tackle Trey Teague was moved to center. Teague and Manning were roommates. Manning was asked if he and Teague had exchanged enough center snaps before the Arkansas game.

"During commercials, we'd get up and I'd take snaps," Manning said. "He got mad at me once because I got him up during the middle of 'Seinfeld'."

Tennessee scored 55 points on Arkansas. The Vols piled up 56 on Kentucky. The Vols struggled to beat Vanderbilt 14-7 to cap a disappointing 9-2 season. They accepted a bid to play Big 10 co-champion Northwestern in the Citrus Bowl.

Manning was dazzling against the Wildcats, throwing for 400 yards, the third time in his career he would reach that milestone.

But it was a 12-yard gain that was the highlight for Manning. It was one of those game-within-a-game plays.

Northwestern's defense was showing a blitz against a run play. Manning checked to a pass. As Northwestern checked out of a blitz, Manning checked back to a run. He handed to Graham, who ran for 12 yards.

"That was my favorite play because I knew I was kind of beating their defensive coordinator on that play," Manning said.

It was another example of Manning being a coach on the field, and another example of why he was ready for the NFL.

Peyton Manning held court, fielding a barrage of questions after his surprising announcement that he would play his senior season at Tennessee. Peyton is flanked by Phillip Fulmer (left) and Archie Manning.

Chapter Six:

The Millions Can Wait

"I wanted to create more memories"
– Peyton Manning

THE BUILDUP WAS OVER. THE DECISION HAD BEEN made. The answer to the most asked question in East Tennessee for several months - would he go or stay? - was moments away.

It was March 5, 1997. Peyton Manning walked into the Ray Mears Room of Thompson-Boling Arena. He was wearing a navy blue sports coat, a light blue shirt, a black and yellow tie and a poker face.

A crowd of more than 150 jammed into the media room. Manning's parents, some teammates, some coaches and some friends were there. Media from New York, New Orleans, Atlanta and *Sports Illustrated* were there. The press conference was such a huge event in Knoxville, television soap operas were preempted. Radio carried it live.

If Manning turned pro, he surely would have been the number one NFL draft pick of the New York Jets and new coach Bill Parcells. If Manning stayed, it would be the biggest upset since the Jets beat the Baltimore Colts in Super Bowl III.

Everyone was curious. A few months before, Archie Manning said he visited the Pope in New Orleans, and the Pope asked: "Is Peyton going to come out this year?"

Tennessee fans feared the worst — for good reason. Not much positive had happened for men's athletics in 24,500-seat Thompson-Boling Arena. Until the 1997-98 season, the men's basketball team had been stuck in idle for the better part of a decade. Just four years earlier, in January 1994, in the exact same room, quarterback Heath Shuler, a Heisman Trophy runner-up and the most beloved of all Vols at the time, announced he was following his dream - not to mention a $19-

million contract - to play in the NFL. Shuler turned pro with one year of eligibility remaining.

Why would Manning do anything different? How could he? The estimated price tag was about $25 million. He had been a starter since the fourth game of his freshman season. He was 28-4 with a helmet full of passing records. And he would have his bachelor's degree in his hip pads.

What more could he want out of college? What more could he achieve? Pro scouts were telling him he was ready for the NFL; he was good enough to be the top pick. He could make all the throws, make all the defensive reads. Besides, just days before, Archie Manning told HBO's "Inside the NFL" that he had a gut feeling his son would turn pro. Vol fans felt rejected by Shuler. They were braced to be rejected by Manning, too.

Manning strolled into the Ray Mears room with head coach Phillip Fulmer, offensive coordinator David Cutcliffe and sports publicist Bud Ford.

The media was abuzz. Manning had told teammates the day before that he was turning pro, the father of a player told me. But if that were true, wouldn't the hard-digging New York media have the scoop? Wouldn't someone have wiggled that information out of a Jets spokesman who talked on the condition he not be identified?

Agent Leigh Steinberg said Manning would stay. Most everyone else thought Manning would go.

Manning took the podium. His voice quivered. He didn't seem this nervous against Florida's blitz.

"I'm not going to try to make this a dramatic ordeal, but there are a few comments I'd like to make," Manning began.

"I guess the one thing that's been running through my mind over and over the past couple of months has been 'Hurry up, and know, Peyton, hurry up and know.' That's what I've been telling myself.

"Yesterday morning (March 4, 1997) I woke up with a huge sense of relief because I finally knew what I was going to do. ... As difficult as it has been, I knew I couldn't make a bad decision, but I knew whatever decision I made had to be my own decision and nobody else's.

Chapter 6 – The Millions Can Wait

"I've thoroughly researched the situation and gathered a great deal of information. I've asked dozens of people what they thought and I have prayed a lot about it also. I knew I wanted to be 100 percent sure of my decision.

"Somebody asked me this morning, what was the one thing that helped sway my opinion and helped me decide. Well, there wasn't one thing. It's just like when I signed here; it was just sort of a feeling.

"I made up my mind and I don't expect to ever look back. I am going to stay at the University of Tennessee."

Thunderous applause erupted. The cheers lasted for more than 30 seconds. Manning had essentially told Tennessee's football program that it meant more to him to stay in college another year than take the money and run. You think that's not a huge endorsement for a football program? You think he didn't endear himself to Tennessee fans forever?

"That surprised me more than the O.J. Simpson verdict," said Tennessee offensive lineman Brad Lampley. "It was one of the most pleasant things that happened to me. We had prepared ourselves so much that he wasn't going to be here."

When the noise died down, Manning said with a smile: "Coach Fulmer just told me I could call my own plays."

Fulmer, feeling the world at his feet, countered: "He's got to win the job in spring practice."

Manning one-upped the coach again: "He promised me books, tuition, food ... and I get to drive his Lexus around the block every now and then."

What more could a college quarterback want?

"I'm so happy for him, knowing that he probably made the right decision," said Olivia Manning, who felt all along Peyton would return to Tennessee. "I don't think money ever played into it. It was staying or going. It was a big decision in his life. But we knew he would make the right one."

Cutcliffe walked up from behind and tapped Manning on the shoulder. "I got three guys off the street I want you to meet," Cutcliffe said. When Manning turned around, he spotted three of his receivers —

Fans and teammates erupt with applause as Manning says he'd rather play another year of college than accept the riches of the NFL.

Marcus Nash, Andy McCullough and Peerless Price — and gave each an emotional hug.

Despite continued prodding, Manning couldn't pinpoint one particular reason why he decided to stay. Did he not want to play for Parcells or the Jets? Was he waiting for the NFL salary cap to be increased? Did he want to return to beat Florida? Win the Heisman Trophy? Win the SEC? Win a national championship?

What was the real reason?

Manning is a guy who leaves no stone unturned. During his recruitment, he could tell you the third-team quarterback at Washington State, for crying out loud. Before a game, he would tell you the height, weight, speed and class of the opposing backup cornerback.

Then he makes the biggest decision of his life based on a feeling?

Manning sought a wide-range of advice. He had more time than usual to study his situation due to an obscure NFL rule that allowed him to wait about two weeks before for the late-April draft to declare. The NFL usually gives an underclassman until Jan. 10 to declare if he will turn pro. That provides the NFL extra time to evaluate the player, and it lets the college know whether it needs to replace the player during recruiting.

But Manning, who crammed his head into books as often as he did game films, was scheduled to graduate in May of 1997, completing his speech communication degree in three years. Thus, staying in college to get a degree would not be an issue. If he stayed, he would play his senior year as a graduate student. And being on course to graduate early bought three more months to decipher what he'd do.

In fairness to Tennessee, he set an unofficial deadline of mid-March, before spring practice began. At times, the extra time added to the frustration.

"The most agonizing thing was being asked so many times what was I going to do," Manning said. "The funny thing is, everybody seemed to know before I made my decision. Everybody had their own ideas, and I kept telling everybody, 'I might stay, just give me a chance, give me a little time.'

"Nobody thought I might stay. Nobody listened to me when I said I didn't know what I was going to do. Everybody thought I was lying just to cover myself and that I was really leaving. That's why they were so surprised and happy, I guess, that I stayed."

With the help of contacts his father arranged, Manning talked to NFL quarterbacks Roger Staubach, Troy Aikman, Drew Bledsoe, Bernie Kosar, Rick Mirer and Phil Simms. He talked to Michael Jordan, Wake Forest basketball All-American Tim Duncan (who completed his eligibility rather than turn pro the year before) and Tennessee Lady Vols basketball coach Pat Summitt.

Jordan told Manning: "Follow your heart and whatever you do will be the right decision."

Summitt said: "My gut feeling was that Peyton didn't want to leave Tennessee. But I didn't know what he would do."

Despite his dogged research, Manning found no magical answer.

"All these pro people said, 'Do what you want, but if it were me, I'd go pro,'" Manning said. "As you look at your list, there are more reasons to go pro than there are to stay."

But there was Michael Jordan advising: Follow your heart. But what was his heart saying? One day, it said go. The next day, it said stay.

Simms, who won a Super Bowl for the New York Giants while playing for Jets coach Bill Parcells, gave a glowing report on Parcells. "Phil Simms couldn't say enough good things about him," Manning said. "He said, 'He's everything you want in a coach. He will protect you. He's going to win.'"

Manning would have a chance to play for a proven NFL coach who had taken three teams to a Super Bowl. Compare that to his father, who, despite being a two-time All-Pro NFL quarterback, never played on a winning team for the New Orleans Saints, never played in a playoff game, never had a top-notch head coach, never had the same offensive coordinator for more than two years. In fact, Archie Manning played for eight offensive coordinators in 11 pro seasons in New Orleans.

Peyton wouldn't have to do that. He wouldn't be subjected to the same frustrations and failures as his father - if he turned pro now; if he were drafted by the Jets.

"How can I turn away from that?" Peyton Manning said of the chance to play for Parcells.

But then, his heart started tugging at him. His parents always told him your college days are the greatest days of your life. You create friends. You create bonds. You create memories.

Many of Archie's best friends were his teammates at Ole Miss from 1967-70. His fondest football memories were at Ole Miss, not in the NFL. Archie's wife, Olivia Williams, was the homecoming queen at Ole Miss. It doesn't get much better than that.

Then came this advice from his mother: "If you're 95 percent sure you want to go pro, then stay. You should be 100 percent sure."

Manning wasn't 100 percent sure. Not even close. Maybe 80-20. Maybe 60-40. But never 100 percent. So, he did what few expected him to do. He stayed in college. "I wanted to create more memories," Manning said. "Staying was strong in my mind and my heart, and that's what I wanted to do."

It was a close call, however.

"I very easily could be sitting here telling everybody that I'm leaving right now, telling everybody good-bye," Manning said. "I thought I could be happy going to the NFL. I'm happy with what I'm doing right now. I was in a win-win situation."

Manning asked himself: "If I turn pro, will I look back?"

The answer: "There's no question, I would have looked back and asked what could I have done my senior year? What did I miss? I didn't want to have that feeling. I didn't want to look back."

Then Manning flashed his sense of humor that he too often hid from the public: "Jim Druckenmiller owes me a cold one." By Manning staying in college one more year, Druckenmiller became the first quarterback taken in the 1997 NFL draft.

Manning's decision to stay at Tennessee put him in position to be a consultant to others. LSU running back Kevin Faulk, who led the SEC in rushing and all-purpose yards last year, deliberated after the 1997 season whether to return for his senior season or turn pro. He called Manning. LSU coach Gerry DiNardo even called Archie Manning to

Peyton Manning had too much fun at Tennessee not to enjoy the fruits of a senior season in college.

discuss Faulk's situation. Faulk stayed at LSU.

Manning said winning the Heisman Trophy, winning the national championship and beating Florida were not factors in his decision.

"Obviously, those things would be nice," Manning said. "But anybody that knows me knows I did not come back here for those three things. I came back because I want to be in college one more year."

Florida coach Steve Spurrier had an intriguing reaction to Manning's announcement.

"Looks like he'll have a chance to become the first three-time MVP of the Florida Citrus Bowl," Spurrier said.

Talk about a dig. In the SEC, the second-best team usually is invited to play in the Florida Citrus Bowl. In Knoxville, it has almost become politically incorrect to say, "Citrus Bowl." It is the SEC runner-up bowl. The second-place bowl. The consolation bracket. Tennessee had played in the Citrus Bowl in 1994, 1996 and 1997. The Vols didn't want to go back. And here was Spurrier, suggesting the Vols were Orlando-bound again, suggesting Florida would again rule in the SEC.

In the irony of all ironies, Florida had the second-best team in the SEC in 1997 and played in the Citrus Bowl. Tennessee won the SEC and played No. 2 Nebraska in the Orange Bowl.

All that was farthest from Manning's mind on March 5, although he knew then Tennessee would be anointed the SEC favorites and that the Vols would be expected to beat Florida - which they didn't.

"I hope we'll have a good team," Manning said. "But I really don't want the fans ... to think, 'Manning is back. We're No. 1.' I'm sure Florida would be laughing at us for saying that."

No matter what the Gators thought, this was a day that would rank among the most satisfying in Tennessee football history. "Thank you, Peyton" billboards sprung up around Knoxville. Fans honked their horns on the highway. Editorials praised him. It was feel-good time in Tennessee, if you were a football fan.

But Manning was reluctant to carry the torch too far. He didn't want his decision to be interpreted as a statement that student-athletes should complete their eligibility. He said he would never blame a college player for turning pro early, especially if he needed financial security. "All situations are unique," Manning insisted.

Manning's is. His family has financial security. Archie did well in the NFL and has done well thereafter. He makes numerous speaking engagements, he endorses several products and he was a radio color analyst for the New Orleans Saints for over 10 years. The Mannings had enough money to pay premiums on a $1 million insurance policy for Peyton's sophomore year, a $5-million- plus policy for his junior season, and a $7 million policy for his senior season.

"Like my father has always said, my mother has a house," Peyton said.

Peyton Manning said he might have turned pro if his family were not well-off financially. Yet, he knew some people would question how in the world he could turn down so much money to be a college quarterback one more year and risk injury, risk not achieving his goals.

"I'm not saying I didn't look at the money," he said. "I'm human. Believe me, I looked at the money. I'm hoping the money will be there next year, too.

"I don't want the NFL people to look at me like, 'He's stupid.' This was my decision. This is what I wanted to do. All people are different."

Some agents thought Peyton was "crazy" to stay in college, Archie Manning said. Parcells might have thought Manning was crazy, too, but he didn't say so.

"I think the common feeling in this country today is that everybody sells out for the money and the opportunity," Parcells said. "I think that in Peyton's case, I admire his decision and think that it took courage to make it, and I wish him well. I am very respectful of his decision, I really am. I think it's refreshing, really."

Some have speculated Manning returned because Parcells wouldn't guarantee to make Manning the first pick. The Mannings deny that. Parcells said he talked to Archie once and they didn't discuss whether the Jets would take Peyton with the first pick.

Manning made it clear he has a strong desire to play in the NFL.

"I want to have a better experience in pro football than I did in college football," he said. "I want pro football, believe me. But I want college football one more year, also.

"I know for a fact I can become a better player. I can get bigger, faster and stronger. I'm going to be a better player next year for whatever team takes me."

Manning said the risk of injury, which would have blown a potentially huge signing bonus and contract with the NFL, was not a concern.

"I play every play, every game as though it might be my last," Manning said, alluding to the career-ending spinal condition of older brother Cooper. "I could be hurt walking to my car after this press conference."

Manning was playing well enough during his junior year to think: this is it. He was leaning toward turning pro. He was on a roll. His team was on a roll.

"I thought I was good enough to come out," he said. "My decision swayed so many times, I figured I was leaving. ... I was proving to myself I was ready to leave."

On the other hand, he thought: "Why am I even considering leaving? I'm having fun. I like what I'm doing. I like the people. I love the fans."

All that good feeling was challenged later in the season. Sailing along at 6-1 and headed to an Alliance bowl if they won, the Vols were upset by Memphis. Memphis? Memphis was a 25-point underdog and had a losing record. Nonetheless, the Vols were stunned by Memphis, 21-17. It was the first time Memphis had ever beaten the Vols in football. And Manning was the quarterback.

"I don't know if I ever felt worse," said Manning, who dragged himself off the field, went into the shower, sat down on a bench and mumbled to himself: "Did this really happen?" He didn't want to leave the dressing room. He didn't want to see the media, his friends, his family. He wanted to stay in the solitude of that losing dressing room, just like a schoolboy who'd been in trouble with his teacher and didn't want to go home to face his parents.

Yet, he said later, the Memphis defeat was not a factor in his decision. He knew what college life was all about. So he promised himself he wouldn't come to a definitive conclusion until he had researched the pro end of it. And that would have to wait until after the bowl game. Still, he knew Tennessee's last home game in 1996 — against Kentucky — could be his last at Neyland Stadium, where an average 106,000 fans showed up each game for four years to watch Manning and the Vols.

Often that last week, it ran through Manning's mind that this might be his college swan song. He also wanted to play well to send the seniors out on a positive note.

So minutes before kickoff, he stood before the team and said: "Being a senior at Tennessee is one of the most special things in the world. We need to send these guys out the right way. This is a special place and it's got to be a great feeling to be a senior and win your last game at home."

Fulmer looked at Manning with a quizzical expression as if to say: "Did I hear Peyton just say that?"

There was no hidden meaning, though. "I didn't think twice about saying it," Manning said. "But it's how I felt. If I were to have left, I'd have missed being a senior at Tennessee."

Fulmer said one of the first things that crossed his mind when Manning was making his decision was: "How am I going to feel when he plays his last game and runs through the 'T' the last time? How much emotion is going to be running through that stadium?"

After Tennessee creamed Kentucky, Manning walked slowly off the field. He looked around the stands. He soaked in the atmosphere. He thought to himself: "This might have been my last time to play here."

And he disappeared under the stands, still wondering.

Manning said before the Citrus Bowl game that it was "possible" he would make a decision before going to Orlando. He'd heard what a distraction it was for the team in December 1993 when Shuler hadn't made up his mind, turning the trip into a media circus. The attention given Shuler stirred some resentment from teammates who felt ignored by the media.

Manning didn't want history to repeat. But he wasn't giving too many hints. His girlfriend of three years, Ashley Thompson of Memphis, would be graduating from the University of Virginia in six more

Tennessee fans display their appreciation for Manning's decision to stay at the 1997 season opener.

months. She asked Peyton where she should apply for a job.

The New York Jets, New Orleans Saints and Atlanta Falcons were battling for the NFL's worst record that year. The worst team would have a chance to draft Manning. So Peyton told Ashley to interview in New York, New Orleans, Atlanta and Knoxville.

"My love of college football is going to have a lot to do with my decision," Manning said in December 1996. "You hear a lot of guys say, 'I have to follow my dream and go play NFL football.' I'm kind of living my dream right now, playing college football.

"Maybe if I hadn't played my freshman year, this wouldn't be as hard a decision. I have played three years, so I have had a good experience playing college football. But I just might come back and play another year because I'm enjoying it so much."

A few days before the Citrus Bowl, Manning offered revealing insight into his future. He had been nominated for an ESPY Award for ESPN's College Play of the Year. It was the time he turned a quarterback sneak into a touchdown pass against Georgia.

"If I come back next year, it'll be to win an ESPY, not the Heisman," Manning joked.

Tennessee overwhelmed Northwestern in the Citrus Bowl. Manning was terrific. He completed 27 of 39 passes for 408 yards and four touchdowns in a 48-28 victory.

Toward the end of the game, Tennessee fans shouted, "One more year, one more year." You could almost hear the chant at Church Street Station, two miles away.

Manning stood on the Vols' bench, facing the fans. He cupped his right ear with his right hand as if to say: "I can't hear you."

"One more year, one more year," fans screamed, louder and louder.

Manning nodded and stepped down from the bench. Was the nod a signal? A sign? Fans wondered. Media wondered. Even teammates wondered. "I was flattered by that," Manning said of the fans. "I enjoyed that moment. ... The fans screwed me up. I was mixed emotionally about what I was going to do."

Olivia said she thought Peyton was influenced by the crowd support. But it wasn't a deciding factor. No, what got him was his mother's advice. If you turn pro, be 100 percent sure.

Rumors were rampant about what Manning might do.

Joe Harrington, Tennessee's visual resource specialist for football, was convinced Manning was turning pro because, after the Citrus Bowl, he hadn't seen Manning in two months. Usually, Manning wants tapes of last year's Tennessee games and next year's Tennessee opponents.

Manning secluded himself from the media as he deliberated. On a trip to New Orleans, he ate lunch with Newman coaches Tony Reginelli and Jeff Brock. A bulletin came on the radio. The Mobile (Ala.) Register reported Manning was turning pro.

"Peyton hadn't made a decision," Brock said. "He hadn't come close."

Chapter 6 – The Millions Can Wait

After weeks of tossing and turning, Manning called his father in New Orleans on March 1 and said that he wanted to stay at Tennessee. No need to rush, said Archie. Sleep on it.

On Monday night, Archie asked: "What do you want to do?"

Peyton: "Dad, I want to sleep on it one more night."

The next morning at 7:45, Manning called his father again.

"Dad, this is what I want to do. This is what I feel in my heart. I'm just lying to myself if I tell myself I don't want to do this."

Peyton told his parents to pack their bags and catch a flight to Knoxville for a March 5 press conference. UT announced a press conference was set. Media began scrambling, trying to break the news. What would Manning do? Manning made himself scarce. And even those that saw him couldn't crack him.

On March 4, Fulmer went to the dining cafeteria at Gibbs Hall, where about half of the student-athletes live. Fulmer sat next to Manning.

"Anything you want to tell me?" Fulmer asked.

"No," Manning said.

"I want to be prepared," Fulmer said.

Manning wouldn't even tell his coach. Fulmer kept steering the conversation toward Manning's decision. Manning wouldn't budge. Was he afraid word would leak out? Did he think Fulmer would leap from the table, creating a scene and thus tipping Peyton's hand? For whatever reason, Manning made Fulmer wait ... until late that night, after the TV news was over, after the newspapers had been put to bed, after the radio talk shows had ended.

At 12:45 a.m., Manning called Fulmer at home, awaking the coach. Fulmer was prepared for the worst.

"I was ready to be knocked to my knees," Fulmer said.

"I'm going to hang around for one more year," Manning said.

"I love you, man," Fulmer said.

After a restless night, Fulmer woke up. He turned to his wife, Vicky, and asked: "Did I dream that last night, or did it really happen?"

It happened.

At the time, Cutcliffe said he was visiting with the Atlanta Falcons about their running game. Cutcliffe figured the Vols were headed for a 60-40 run-pass ratio if Manning left. Cutcliffe had a more positive feeling intuitively that Manning would sign with Tennessee in 1994 than he now had about Manning staying for his senior season.

"I can't say I felt good about this one," Cutcliffe said. "He's older now and he's got a little bit better poker face than he had."

When Manning broke the news to Cutcliffe, he had one question: "Are you kidding?"

Assured that Manning wasn't, Cutcliffe spent a sleepless night. How could he sleep with all those pass patterns flying through his head?

Manning shocked Tennessee fans when he announced on March 5, 1997, that he would return for his senior season at Tennessee, even though he had his college degree. No one was happier about the decision than Vols coach Phillip Fulmer.

Peyton Manning took head coach Phillip Fulmer on a Rocky Top high during his brilliant Tennessee career. In 1997, Manning helped Tennessee win their first SEC Championship since 1990. Manning set 33 school, seven SEC and two NCAA records.

Chapter Seven:

An Unbelievable Experience

"I wouldn't change one thing"
— *Peyton Manning*

IF YOU LOOKED CLOSELY FROM THE SIDELINE, YOU might recognize her. She was standing near second base, interviewing Peyton Manning.

It had come to this.

It wasn't enough that ABC, CBS, ESPN, Fox "Sports South" and *Sports Illustrated* had spent enough time in Knoxville to pay property taxes, but here was another media angle.

Paula Zahn of CBS News' "This Morning" was in Knoxville to talk to Peyton during two-a-day practices at the baseball stadium in August of his senior season. She was doing a story about the impact Manning's decision to stay at Tennessee would have on other athletes.

The publicity generated by Manning for Tennessee was unprecedented. He was on scores of magazine covers. He did public service announcements: Learn to read; Wear a helmet when you ride a bike. He did one spot with police chief Phil Keith that took longer than expected because Keith couldn't remember his lines.

"The media is something my dad told me to get ready for if I wanted to be a good player at a major-college program like Tennessee," Peyton said. "You might as well accept it. I've always had good experiences with the media."

Being interviewed, Manning said, is just part of the job.

"I've enjoyed getting to know a lot of members of the media and doing it the right way," Manning said. "You're doing interviews with the media, but you're doing interviews with the fans, too. You're letting them get to know you. I wanted people to see me the right way."

Expectations for Manning's senior season with the Vols weren't as outrageous as they were for his junior season. Yet, some hoped that maybe, somehow, the Vols could unseat Florida as the SEC champions.

Only days before the season began, a bombshell hit. The University of Tennessee agreed to pay former associate trainer Dr. Jamie Whited, $300,000 to settle 33 sexual harassment charges against the athletic department, the maximum dollar amount allowable in the state of Tennessee.

A UT trainer for nine years (1988-96), Whited, a woman, took a five-months leave of absence in the spring of 1996 after witnessing a Manning mooning in the training room Feb. 29 of that year. Manning was standing up while Whited was examining his ankle. Manning said he dropped his drawers to moon a track athlete, Malcolm Saxon of Memphis. Whited argued Manning was mooning her, because her face was less than two feet from his buttocks when the mooning occurred.

Two weeks after the mooning, a man called Mike Keith's "SportsTalk" show on a Knoxville radio station to ask about the incident. Many dismissed it as a prank call. It wasn't until May 2 that it hit *The Knoxville News-Sentinel.*

"I was clowning around in the training room with a good friend of mine and she happened to see it," said Manning, who wanted to make a public statement at the time against his father's advice. "By no means was anything directed at her. It was nothing more than a joke toward somebody else. My practical jokes have come to an end."

Whited wouldn't comment. She referred all questions to Tennessee athletic director Doug Dickey.

So, Manning's version of the story was made public. Whited's was not. Whited was ticked. In the ensuing weeks, Whited was ridiculed on radio talk shows and in the print media. Few people sided publicly with a woman in a predominantly male setting. The prevailing opinion: If seeing a man's butt traumatized her, then get the hell out of the training room and the training profession. Surely, she had seen half of a man's rear cheek before.

In fact, she had. About two years before the Manning incident, a baseball player mooned Whited. Whited filed no complaint. Which begs the question: Why would Whited be torn apart by a Manning mooning, yet not even report a similar act by a no-name athlete? Some felt Whited knew she wouldn't get attention complaining about Joe Blow, but she would about Peyton Manning.

According to sources, Manning was surprised that Whited was offended by the mooning and dismissed her objections. The night of the mooning, Tennessee trainer Mike Rollo was notified of the incident. He went to visit Whited, then Manning. Not until then did Manning realize the potential ramifications.

Whited was perceived by many as "one of the guys." She cursed. She told dirty jokes. She talked "gutter" talk. Manning thought it would be extra funny if he mooned Saxon behind Whited's back. But even if she happened to see him, Manning didn't think Whited would care. She could take a joke, he thought. He was wrong.

Manning considered the mooning a childish prank, something older brother Cooper did all the time. Whited considered it sexual harassment.

Manning called Whited to apologize. Her husband, John Whited, answered the phone but wouldn't let Manning talk to her. He then sent a registered letter apologizing. Still no response from Whited.

Whited, who married the son of a former head baseball coach at Tennessee, did not believe Manning was sincere in his apology. She also chided the Knoxville media for protecting Manning, saying the national media did a better job exposing what had happened. She charged that Manning had the local media fooled and that he was really the opposite of his good-guy image.

Whited claimed that Manning's version of what happened was a fabrication, but she wouldn't describe the incident in detail. She did, however, make it clear that she felt the mooning was directed at her, not the track athlete.

Manning was punished for the mooning by Fulmer. Manning was made to run at 6 a.m. and was taken off the training table for the rest of the spring semester. The Mannings were fuming. They thought the punishment was excessive. "Peyton admitted to me he was wrong," Archie said. "But I'm not sure his punishment didn't outdo the crime.

"I felt for him in this case because what happened took place away from the public. Peyton felt a little betrayed by her (Whited) because he'd done a favor for her by doing a speaking engagement one time when she asked him."

Cutcliffe was assigned to supervise the runs. Manning spent most of his time doing passing drills.

Manning didn't like the idea of getting up before sunrise, but he was really mad about the training-table discipline. He wasn't eating right. He was losing weight. After a week or so, he went to Fulmer and charged that the punishment was too severe. The early-morning runs were stopped and Manning went back to the training table.

Not long after Whited lodged the complaint, Manning called Saxon to make sure he would support Peyton's story. Saxon said if he were asked, he wasn't sure what he'd say. Manning feared Saxon might say Manning was mooning Whited, not Saxon.

Growing enraged, Manning talked to his father about applying for the supplemental draft in the summer of 1996.

Because of Whited's extended leave, Dickey was asked if something was wrong with Whited's health: "She says so," he replied.

When Tim Layden of *Sports Illustrated* came to Knoxville to do a feature, Manning was worried about how Layden would handle the mooning in the magazine's preseason football issue. Layden detailed the incident, but wrote only a few paragraphs.

Whited returned in August of 1996. I was covering practice that day, but I went into Whited's office to see her. She wouldn't talk about the incident on the record. I told her that based on what I thought had happened, she overreacted. She defended herself and said I didn't know the whole story, but she wouldn't tell me her version of the whole story.

After an hour of talking, I went to practice.

After practice, Fulmer pulled me aside and asked me if he should know anything about my talk with Whited. Somehow he knew I had visited her. Fulmer seemed concerned that Whited might file some type complaint that would force Manning to miss, say, the Florida game the next month. I told him I knew of no such plan.

It wasn't until a year later — August 1997 — that Whited and the University of Tennessee reached a settlement. Part of the agreement forbade Whited from talking about her complaints.

Three media members waited after practice that day to get Manning's reaction about the settlement, which was released by the University of Tennessee late on a Friday afternoon.

"I'm glad it's all behind me, no pun intended," said Manning, who then hopped in a truck driven by his girlfriend and headed back to the dressing room.

Tennessee players were told not to talk about the case with the media. University of Tennessee officials were not to be found that Friday afternoon. They left their offices to avoid fielding questions.

What they did was a total disservice to Manning. They let the media think Whited's case was solely about the Manning mooning. Headlines across the country blared: "Trainer Gets $300,000 for Manning Mooning." Some media suggested Manning should be forced to cover the $300,000 expense.

In truth, the Manning mooning was just one of 33 complaints that the two parties publicly acknowledged, whittled down from more than 300 Whited actually filed. Had all of Whited's claims been made public, some high-ranking officials in the Tennessee athletic department could have been fired for sexual harassment, insensitive jokes and off-color remarks, according to sources.

UT agreed to pay the $300,000 to resolve the matter. But UT officials left Manning hanging. To his credit, Manning never blasted the University of Tennessee for leaving him high and dry. But it wasn't exactly the way he envisioned the start of his final season. If the settlement served as a distraction to Manning, you couldn't tell it. He tied a school record, passing for five touchdowns in the season opener against Texas Tech, which was two years removed from the Cotton Bowl.

Co-captains Peyton Manning and Leonard Little pose next to Tennessee's 1951 national championship trophy. They had visions of bringing another national title to Tennessee before the '97 season.

The next week, Manning had 341 passing yards in a close victory at UCLA. Tennessee led 24-3 and held on for a 30-24 win.

"The locker room was like a morgue," Manning said. "It's a shame it was that way. In the NFL, you take a close win like that and you're celebrating and high-fiving. We acted like we'd lost."

After an open date, Tennessee would face Florida in the fourth and final showdown of Manning's career. Manning was 0-2 as a starter against the Gators. Beating Florida was one of the few things Manning had not accomplished in his college career. He'd beaten Alabama. He'd won a big bowl game over a No. 4 ranked team. He'd had a pair of 400-yard passing games.

But he'd never beaten Florida.

Many felt the Florida game would define his Tennessee career.

"People were saying, 'Can he beat Florida?' I didn't like that at all. I didn't see it that way," said Manning, perturbed at the Manning v. Florida hype. "The simple fact is, if you don't play well enough, you won't beat them."

Once again, Tennessee didn't play well enough. Florida scored the first two touchdowns, with Tony George returning an errant Manning pass 89 yards for a touchdown. In control all the way, Florida won 33-20 as Manning had a subpar game and UT's offensive line was pathetic.

After the final horn, Manning saw Florida coach Steve Spurrier near midfield.

"He gives you a handshake and he never looks you in the eyes," Manning said. "I've always respected Coach Spurrier as a coach. I think some of the things he says I don't think he should say."

Manning left Florida Field slowly, perhaps sore from the beating he'd taken, perhaps knowing this was his last chance to beat hated Florida, to beat the fans who hung him in effigy before the game. Gator fans were dogging Manning.

"It wasn't much fun," Manning said.

After the bitter defeat, Manning was asked where Tennessee goes from here: "People are going to make jokes and things like that, but we still have plenty to play for." The jokes would be about another return trip

Manning didn't get protection like this very often against Florida. Manning never beat the Gators as a starter, losing three of his six career games to Florida.

to the Citrus Bowl. You know the one about how you can't spell citrus without UT.

Then, Manning took the game on his shoulders: "I apologize to the fans and the coaches and the people who wanted this game so badly for not getting the job done."

Manning might not have played his best, but he certainly wasn't the main reason Tennessee lost. The Vols abandoned the running game too quickly against Florida, didn't have answers for the Gators' zone blitz, and used too much single coverage in the secondary on Florida's best receiver, Jacquez Green.

"I screwed that game up so bad," Cutcliffe said, "nobody could fix it."

But it was Manning after the game, apologizing for the defeat.

"The reason I apologized is, I'd like to have done my part a little bit better," Manning said. "I realize I couldn't beat them on my own, but I could have helped my team win.

"Fans had talked about that game all season long. They said, 'Peyton, we're going to get Florida this year.' You want to win for those people, and the fans who made the trip down there. I wanted to do my part better."

He added: "I was mad, but we had to move on. We could have a lot more fun this year and if we were to possibly win the SEC Championship, it would, at least this year, negate the loss to Florida."

SEC Championship? Yeah, right.

Tennessee had been in this position before, several times. The Vols waited and hoped for a Florida loss. But Florida hadn't lost in the SEC since 1994. What were the chances this year? Slim to none.

Manning was afraid Tennessee would still be suffering from a Florida hangover. The Vols had to live with the pasting at Florida for an extra week because of an open date before playing Ole Miss.

Ole Miss might not excite a receiver from Oklahoma or a lineman from North Carolina, but it excited Manning. The initial shock of playing his father's alma mater was gone, but there was still the Rebel flag, still the blue and red, still hoddy toddy, and he was still the son of Ole Miss' greatest player.

"A lot of guys were believing the Citrus Bowl is where we were headed," Manning said. "So you had to work even harder to get fired up. You had to be creative."

Moments before the heavily favored Vols took the field at Neyland Stadium against the Rebels, Manning addressed the team. Nobody wanted to hear a pep talk. Manning talked anyway.

"Hey seniors, this is it for a lot of us," he said. "The NFL is no fun. If I score, I'm going to jump into the stands like the Green Bay Packers. Let's play loose and have fun."

Tennessee won 31-17 and Manning had 324 passing yards.

But the story of the day was a freshman running back named Jamal Lewis. In his first start, the 230-pounder from Atlanta rushed for 155 yards. Manning had another toy to play with.

"Going into that season, we were hoping the running game might appear sometime," Manning said. "We were hoping we could do without it, but knowing deep down it (SEC title) wasn't going to happen unless we found a running game."

Lewis proved he wasn't a one-game wonder. The next week, against Georgia, Lewis piled up 232 yards. Only three backs in Tennessee history rushed for more yards in a single game.

The year before, the Bulldogs opted to recruit another top-notch running back in the state of Georgia, Jasper Sanks. While many recruiting services ranked Sanks ahead of Lewis, who was projected as a full back by some, Sanks did not qualify academically.

After Tennessee defeated Georgia 38-13, Georgia athletic director Vince Dooley was heard to say in the press box elevator: "I hope Jasper Sanks is as good as Jamal Lewis."

Lewis' emergence energized Tennessee.

"It really took a lot of pressure off me," Manning said. "It put me back in the offense I was used to running. Opponents respected the run. So we could set them up with the run and beat them with the pass, or set them up with the pass and beat them with the run.

"I was back in my comfort zone, and I started playing better football from that point on. It allowed me to use my knowledge and experience to the fullest extent, and we ended up winning the rest of our (regular-season) games."

The win over Georgia would be Tennessee's most complete performance of the season.

"It was a perfect illustration of how good we could be when we had a running game and a passing game," Manning said after the Vols rolled up 628 yards against the SEC's top-ranked defense entering the game.

Not only did the Vols get a lift from Lewis, they got hope from LSU. That night, the Tigers upset Florida in Baton Rouge, La., opening a crack in the door for the East Division title. If LSU could beat Florida, maybe Auburn or Georgia could, too.

The next week, Tennessee scored a comfortable 38-21 victory over outmanned Alabama at Legion Field in Birmingham. Manning became the first quarterback ever to beat the Crimson Tide three times. He also became a conductor.

In the post-game mayhem, Manning threw his sweat bands and towels into the crowd. Then, as he prowled the end zone, celebrating with Vol fans, UT's band leader passed the baton.

"It's my senior year," Manning said. "I'm never going to have a chance to do it again. Sure, I'm going to direct the band when the band leader asked me. I didn't hesitate at all. I climbed up there and threw the guy off (the ladder)." What if Manning had been asked in 1994 or 1995 to direct the band? "No way," he said. "In 1994 and 1995, I was trying to develop an image."

Manning noticed the band was in rhythm without his direction, so he started waving to family and friends in the stands.

"That was special," Manning said. "How many people can say they directed the UT band?"

It was another reminder for Manning that he had made the right decision to return to Tennessee.

"Where would I be if I decided to leave?" Manning said. "I sure wouldn't be directing a college band at this point and I surely couldn't be enjoying myself as much as I am now."

In the post-game press conference, Manning wore a T-shirt that said:

Manning directed the Tennessee band in a version of ``Rocky Top'' at Birmingham's Legion Field after the Vols beat rival Alabama for the third straight year.

"Waitin' on Peyton!" in crimson colors. He found it in his locker when he arrived at Legion Field.

"It's special to say you played in that game three straight years," Manning said. "To say you've beaten them the last three years is even more special."

Two weeks later, the red-hot Vols faced South Carolina. The game was significant for two reasons. First, South Carolina quarterback Anthony Wright tore his anterior cruciate ligament and missed the rest of the season. Second, Manning had his worst game of the season, going 8 of 25 for 126 yards with one interception as the Vols squeaked out a 22-7 win.

After the game, Archie advised Peyton not to take blame - like he did after the Florida game - because the Vols won. So when Peyton was asked about his performance, he said: "I thought I played well."

Archie rolled his eyes: "That's not exactly what I meant."

The next week, Manning was sensational against Southern Miss, completing 35 of 53 passes for 399 yards and four touchdowns against a Top 25 team.

The Vols struggled to beat Arkansas in Little Rock with Manning throwing three touchdowns to spark the victory. Arkansas led 22-17 early in the fourth quarter. Manning knew what Tennessee fans were thinking: "Here's the Memphis of '97."

Instead, Manning threw a 49-yard touchdown pass to Marcus Nash on third-and-9. A blocked punt led to a decisive score that gave Tennessee a 30-22 victory.

Then came a much anticipated shootout against Kentucky. It pitted the two best offenses in the SEC and two of the top four quarterbacks in the nation: Manning and Tim Couch.

Manning had a field day. He completed 25 of 35 passes for a school-record 523 yards in a 59-31 victory. As he left the field, Manning was greeted by Archie.

"You couldn't get 17 more yards?" Archie said with a smile.

Actually, Peyton needed 31 more yards. Archie holds the SEC record for total offense in a game with 540, compiled against Alabama during a 33-32

Manning found South Carolina a feisty foe. He hit 8 of 25 passes, but said he played well because Tennessee won.

loss in 1969. Peyton's 509 total yards are the fifth-most by an SEC player and the 523 passing yards are the second-most by an SEC player.

Couch was no slouch. He passed for 476 yards and two touchdown as Kentucky rolled up 634 total yards, the most ever allowed by a Tennessee defense.

"I can't lie," Manning said. "I really enjoyed myself that day."

For the second year in a row, Tennessee had trouble beating Vanderbilt as Commodore coach Woody Widenhofer devised another terrific game plan. The Commodores would show certain defense, inducing Manning to audible to the play they wanted him to run. "You couldn't do that at a lot of schools, but our players were so smart," Widenhofer said. But the 17-10 victory was enough to propel Tennessee into the SEC Championship game for the first time.

The Vols staged an impromptu victory lap inside Neyland Stadium. Players carried the state flag around the field. And Manning, once again, directed Tennessee's band.

Manning grabbed a field microphone and said: "I just want to say thank y'all from the bottom of my heart and from the seniors' hearts. ... Let's go to Atlanta and get Auburn. Let's go baby."

In high school, Manning never won a state championship in football. In college, he'd not won the Eastern Division of the SEC until his senior season. Soon, he would be playing in his first SEC Championship game.

"I was the most excited I'd ever been for a football game in my life," Manning said.

On game day, Auburn arrived at the Georgia Dome before Tennessee. The Tigers took their time getting off the team buses. Manning estimated it at 30 minutes.

"They were doing it on purpose," Manning said. "It was driving me crazy."

Tennessee's first half performance drove Vol fans crazy. The Vols had six turnovers and six dropped passes. Auburn scored on a fumble recovery return and a blocked extra point. Tennessee's comedy of errors wasn't funny to Manning.

Manning had a field day against Kentucky, passing for a school-record 523 yards and five touchdowns. He almost broke the SEC record of 540 total yards, held by his father.

Manning makes his final walk to Neyland Stadium, then walks off the field with a raised fist as Tennessee won its first-ever SEC East Division title.

In the second half, Manning threw a pass to Jeremaine Copeland inside the Auburn 10-yard line. Copeland bobbled the pass to Auburn defensive back Jayson Bray, who made a 77-yard interception return.

Manning's right knee bounced off the artificial turf as he tried to flag down Bray. It wasn't until several hours after the game that Manning knew the extent of what had happened. He had ruptured the bursa sac on his right knee. It eventually became infected and swollen. He could hardly get his pants over his grapefruit-sized knee.

But Manning didn't miss a snap during the game. He played through what he thought was an abrasion. Despite the follies of his teammates, Manning refused to lose. He passed for 373 yards and four touchdowns as Tennessee overcame a 6-1 turnover deficit to down Auburn 30-29.

"It was like we tried to give the game away, tried to lose to a team we were much better than," Manning said.

But Tennessee prevailed and by doing so, captured its first SEC title since 1990.

In the post-game press conference, Manning walked to the podium, spotted his parents in the back of the room, flashed a smile and gave his dad a thumbs up. During the Auburn game, Manning became the SEC's all-time passing leader with 11,201 yards. He had thrown for more yards than Joe Namath, Ken Stabler, Steve Spurrier, Bert Jones, Pat Sullivan, Danny Wuerffel, Eric Zeier ....and Archie Manning.

"It's a great honor just to be mentioned with those names," Manning said.

And at last, the championship ring Manning had sought since his sophomore season at Newman High was his to wear.

Manning had engineered Tennessee to its first appearance in the Bowl Alliance/Bowl Coalition. The No. 3 ranked Vols played No. 2 Nebraska in the Orange Bowl. A Michigan loss to Washington State in the Rose Bowl the day before and a Tennessee win over Nebraska would give the Vols their first national championship since 1951.

That wasn't utmost on Manning's mind. Getting healthy was. Manning had missed just one day of practice in three previous years at Tennessee. But he didn't practice at all during pre-Christmas bowl workouts because of the inflamed knee.

Chapter 7 – An Unbelievable Experience

He was admitted to St. Mary's Hospital in Knoxville, where he stayed for five days. It wasn't your typical stay. Joe Harrington, a tall, lanky lad who is the athletic department's visual resource specialist for football, had his picture made a few months earlier at picture day, wearing a Tennessee jersey but no helmet. He posed like a quarterback. To amuse Manning, Harrington autographed the 8-inch-by-10-inch glossy and brought it to Manning's hospital room.

Manning thought it was hilarious.

Harrington wore No. 8 for photo day, in honor of his good friend Andy Kelly, a former Tennessee quarterback. One well-wisher was fooled by the photo. Chris Cutcliffe, 10-year-old son of offensive coordinator David Cutcliffe, thought the photo was of Kelly.

Manning had one unfortunate incident when a nurse awakened him at 7 a.m. for an autograph. After that, the hospital stationed a security guard at Manning's room to keep away unwelcome visitors. Later, Harrington and Cutcliffe went by to see Manning.

"Who are you guys?" the security guard asked.

"I don't know if you recognize me," Harrington said, "but I'm the guy in the picture by his bed."

Manning's hospital room was like a fast-food restaurant. Friends brought him hamburgers and french fries and other junk food. Manning seldom ate the hospital food.

That prompted an unexpected visit from an offended party. "I'll fix the food the way you want it," said the head chef of St. Mary's Hospital. Manning apologized, afraid he had hurt the chef's feelings for not eating his food.

When Manning was released from the hospital, he went straight to the practice field and rode around briefly in a golf cart. The knee was still huge. An attempt to drain it was unsuccessful. Manning was so unsure of playing in the Orange Bowl, he packed clothes to wear on the sideline just in case.

Michigan destroyed Tennessee's dream scenario by beating Washington State on Jan. 1. Nebraska destroyed Tennessee the next night as a limping Manning finished his college career on a sad, but classy, note. Despite his discomfort, Manning made his way to Nebraska's dressing room to congratulate Cornhuskers coach Tom Osborne, who was retiring after a distinguished 25-year tenure that featured three national championships.

To Manning, the SEC championship capped his season and his career, not the Orange Bowl.

"For me personally, it was an unbelievable experience," he said. "If I went back and did it again, I wouldn't change one thing."

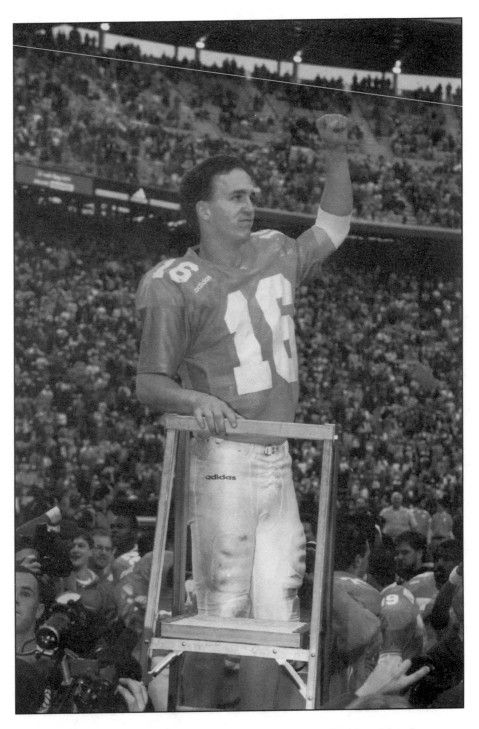

After Tennessee beat Vanderbilt to win the SEC Eastern Division, Manning directed the UT band in his last home game.

Peyton Manning posed with the Heisman Trophy at the Downtown Athletic Club in New York. But he didn't get to take home the hardware. Instead, he became the fourth Vol to finish second in the Heisman race.

Chapter Eight:

The "Heist-man" Trophy

"I never knew what they were looking for..."

– Peyton Manning

THE INTENSITY HAD BUILT TO A CRESCENDO. THE moment had arrived.

Arguably the nation's most prestigious individual award was minutes away from being announced.

History would follow the Heisman Trophy winner forever, like it has followed Paul Hornung and Roger Staubach, Gary Beban and O.J. Simpson, Jim Plunkett and Tony Dorsett.

The winner on Dec. 13 would join select company. Only 51 former Heisman winners are still alive. They are the only non-media members allowed to vote for the outstanding college football player in the country. They are invited each year to join the ceremony.

Who would be the new member? Would it be Tennessee's record-breaking quarterback Peyton Manning, perhaps the most written about and well known college athlete of all time? Or would it be versatile Charles Woodson of Michigan, applauded for making big plays in big games, trumpeted as the best athlete on the No. 1 ranked team in the nation?

Various media members, mostly based in Tennessee, Michigan and New York, debated the outcome for more than two hours in a small media room at the Downtown Athletic Club in New York City. A young man who worked odd jobs at the Downtown Athletic Club professed to have inside information. It was Manning, he said, based on media information disseminated in the room.

Could he be right? Did he have some insight? Did his logic add up? Had he sneaked a peak at the final results in a back room somewhere?

It only added to the intrigue.

The night before, Archie Manning prepared his son for the possibility of not winning the Heisman. His son already had doubts. During the season, Peyton Manning thought he would win. But as days went by, his optimism faded.

ESPN carried the drama for nearly 50 minutes before Downtown Athletic Club president Peter A. Junge opened the envelop.

"And the winner is (pause) from the University of Michigan, Charles Woodson."

Media members covering the event were stunned. They had witnessed the greatest upset in the history of the Heisman Trophy. Manning, sitting beside Woodson at the ceremonies, was the first to shake hands with the Michigan star. A picture of a forlorn looking Manning was splashed across several newspapers. Manning said he wasn't disappointed about not winning the Heisman. The photo said otherwise.

Olivia Manning didn't hide her despair. She cried.

Bud Ford, Tennessee's sports information director who had invested so much time in helping Manning win the Heisman, was heart broken.

"I'm a loser," he said, tears in his eyes. He took the outcome personally, partly because he had become so personally fond of Manning. Virtually the entire state of Tennessee had become fond of Manning. He was the favorite son. And the son didn't win.

"Heist-man Trophy," blared headlines at various Tennessee newspapers.

At the post-announcement press conference, Manning apologized to Tennessee's fans for not bringing the school its first Heisman Trophy winner. He joined a list of three other former Vols who finished second: Hank Lauricella (1951), Johnny Majors (1956) and Heath Shuler (1993).

Tennessee fans are still stung by the fact Majors lost to the only player to have won from a team that had a losing record. Notre Dame was 2-8 the year Hornung beat out Majors.

Heisman Trophy finalists Charles Woodson of Michigan, Peyton Manning of Tennessee, Randy Moss of Marshall and Ryan Leaf of Washington State pose in front of the most recognizable trophy in college sports before the Heisman winner is announced on December 13, 1997. Manning's facial expression makes you think he knew the outcome beforehand.

Now, an even greater UT legend had lost to the first Heisman winner whose primary position was defense.

"I'd be less than honest if I said I didn't want to win this award for the people back home in Tennessee," Manning said that night. "In a lot of ways, I wanted to win it for them because they've been so supportive throughout my four years. I apologize to them."

The news hit Knoxville hard. Fans booed the decision, flipped off their television sets in anger, ripped the Heisman voting process and began a campaign to alter the balloting so another deserving candidate like Manning wouldn't, in their eyes, get robbed.

Manning had touched the lives of a cross section of people by his exploits on the field and his community service off the field. Doctors. Lawyers. Teachers. Second-graders. Members of the Boys & Girls Club of Greater Knoxville. Church groups. Four-H Clubs.

All of them admired Manning, the person and the performer. He was the greatest player in Tennessee history. The most popular. A model citizen. A positive influence on the community. How could he not win the Heisman Trophy?

Knoxville radio station WIVK-WNOX printed 1600 T-shirts with the simple inscription: "Keep Your Stupid Trophy," charged $5 apiece and sold out in less than two hours. A Knoxville novelty shop took over the project and sold another 1,500. The station and novelty shop raised $5,000 for Dream Connection, which helps children with grave illnesses realize their dreams. Several dream requests have been to meet none other than Peyton Manning.

Tennessee head coach Phillip Fulmer and Tennessee offensive coordinator David Cutcliffe were bitter about the Heisman outcome.

"I don't understand," Fulmer said, expressing the views of thousands of Volunteer fans. "But that's the way it is. What a deserving cap it would have been to such a wonderful career."

Cutcliffe was angry and disappointed. But as he watched Manning sign autographs, answer questions and show maturity well beyond his 21 years, Cutcliffe said: "I admire him more than ever for the way he's handling it. He's defying all odds."

Cutcliffe had been to the Heisman ceremonies in 1993 with Shuler.

David Cutcliffe (right) presents Peyton with another award at the Tennessee football banquet.

Shuler wasn't expected to win it and didn't. The award went to Florida State's Charlie Ward. You heard no griping, no complaining from Tennessee fans or coaches. But this was different. Manning not winning was seen as a major injustice, a tragedy.

Fulmer had said before the announcement that voting for Manning was "a no brainer."

Michigan coach Lloyd Carr took offense. But based on Manning's achievements, based on previous results that favored an offensive player, based on the front-runner holding his ground, Fulmer was right.

"I'm not real excited about getting back to New York anytime soon," Cutcliffe said. "It's an interesting phenomenon, what happened this year. I can't explain it, but it bothers me a little bit, the way it occurred."

It bothered others as well.

Former Notre Dame coach Lou Holtz, a CBS analyst in 1997, was critical of the voting.

"I felt it was a disservice to college football and to Peyton Manning," Holtz said. "He did everything a front-runner should do. He set all kinds of records. He led his team to a conference championship. Then all of the sudden, he doesn't win it.

"I hate to say this, but I think it was sort of, 'You've had too many good things happen to you; it's time to have some adversity.' I can't account for anything else."

CBS football announcer Tim Brando said the decision taints the Heisman forever in his mind. He blamed the media for orchestrating an "absolute campaign" to make the Heisman a race and seeking out a versatile defensive player to challenge Manning after Tennessee lost to Florida in September.

"There were some self-absorbed television talking heads and former Heisman Trophy winners high-fiving and back-slapping behind closed doors, congratulating each other for altering the landscape of the Heisman voting forever," said Brando. "Voters couldn't take credit for Peyton Manning winning. They could take credit for Charles Woodson winning."

Brando, who voted Manning first, Leaf second and Marshall receiver Randy Moss third, was shocked that the West Coast vote favored Woodson over Leaf, shocked that Woodson won so easily.

"I don't understand how the media bought into it," Brando said. "It certainly soured me on the Heisman."

ESPN's Mike Gottfried, a former head coach at Kansas and Pittsburgh, said the media was responsible for robbing Manning of the Heisman Trophy. "I don't think there's any doubt Peyton Manning was the best player in the country," Gottfried said. "You can say NFL draft day is different, but to me, the best player was the No. 1 draft pick. (Manning was the first pick and Woodson the fourth pick.)

"The SEC is by far the toughest conference in the country, and what Peyton Manning did in his career factors into the equation. He carried his team. And the way he handled not winning the Heisman Trophy was a Heisman-winning performance. He never moaned, never complained. He set an example on and off the field."

Like Brando and Gottfried, Cutcliffe pointed an accusing finger at the media. "For the media to sit there and tell him, 'We expect you to win it, you should win it, you're the man,' and for Peyton to never, ever do anything to relinquish it, what message is that sending?" Cutcliffe said.

"If you're Peyton Manning, those people who jumped off the bandwagon for no apparent reason don't need to try to jump back on his because I don't think he should forget - or will forget."

Manning's teammates were livid. "I guess we should have thrown (Tennessee cornerback) Terry Fair a few screen passes," said Vols center Trey Teague, mocking Woodson's versatility. "Around here, Peyton is our Heisman winner."

Then, Teague added: "I think it was ridiculous. I can't understand what people were thinking. I don't think the Heisman will mean what it used to, from this point."

Frank Gendusa, Manning's offensive coordinator at Newman High school, was livid. "If you want the best athlete on the field, how could it not be Peyton?" Gendusa said. "If you want honor and integrity and character, how could it not be Peyton?

"It was a slap in the face. It was really disappointing. I just thought they blew it. They had a chance to make a statement that this is what college football is all about. Whether it was politics or color or whatever, I don't know. But I lost a lot of respect for the Heisman Trophy.

"I don't give a rat's tootie about who wins it next year. I don't care about the preseason favorite. I used to be glued to my TV to watch the ceremonies, but I won't ever watch it again."

Gendusa reaches across his office and pulls a book out of a book shelf. He flips open the pages. He pulls out an invitation to a $250 a plate Heisman Awards dinner held two nights after the Heisman selection is announced to honor the winner. The ticket is unused.

Gendusa eagerly anticipated making the trip to New York in hopes of celebrating Manning's Heisman victory. Instead, the ticket rests between the pages of a paperback book as a stark reminder of what might have been.

When Manning left the podium following the Heisman press conference, he walked to the left where a barrage of media converged.

"Bud," Peyton told Tennessee's sports information director, "I'd like to get out of here pretty soon."

Manning was feeling the pain of losing college's most coveted award. He was still feeling the pain of the infected right knee that he hurt Dec. 6. He had a noticeable limp.

"OK," Bud Ford said.

But there was no getting Manning out of the Downtown Athletic Club soon. Woodson won the Heisman, but Manning not winning was the bigger story. He was the season-long favorite until the last month. Manning played the marquee position. He had marvelous numbers. His team won the Southeastern Conference championship for the first time since 1990. He set 42 school, SEC and NCAA records.

And he didn't win the Heisman.

"For me personally, I was not into this award," said Manning, who finished sixth in the Heisman voting in 1996 and eighth in 1997.

Manning was into the award in 1996. He was listed among the top five

Newman coach Frank Gendusa would have worn a bigger smile had Manning won the Heisman. Gendusa keeps an unused ticket to the Heisman awards dinner between the pages of a book in his office as a reminder of what might have been.

in the weekly Scripps Howard Heisman Trophy poll in late October. He had visions of attending the Heisman ceremony. What a great experience it would be, he thought. But a couple of unimpressive games in November cost him a chance to be invited to the awards' ceremony.

In 1997, he was the Heisman favorite until he threw four interceptions in the first half against Florida, and the Gators surged to a 35-0 lead after 20 minutes. A Tennessee rally fell short; the Vols lost 35-29. And even though Manning passed for a school-record 492 yards, Florida's Wuerffel, who was 11 of 22 for 155 yards and five touchdowns, leaped ahead of Manning in the Heisman chase.

"One bad half," Manning said, "and I fall off the books."

Manning still had a shot to finish in the top five, but poor outings in a loss at Memphis and in a close victory over Vanderbilt plummeted him to eighth. No ticket to New York, again.

Though he was reluctant to say so publicly, that chapped Manning. He felt he should have been invited to the Heisman show, and the snub left a sour taste in his mouth. He questioned the process. As Manning said in New York on Dec. 13, 1997, "For the past three years, it's been with me. There hasn't been a day gone by without someone asking me about the Heisman Trophy. Hopefully, now those questions will stop."

Then, he added: "I really don't envy whoever is the preseason favorite next year. I had fun this year, but you've got to work at it. ... People are going to knock you down and pick at you. It's a challenge to have thick skin. If you let it get to you, it can really bother you."

Manning said the Heisman didn't serve as a distraction his senior season because he was prepared for it. "I wasn't going to let it bother me," he said.

Forty-four percent of the votes were cast in the last week. Manning supporters hoped that would work in Manning's favor because he led Tennessee to the SEC championship on Dec. 6. It didn't.

"Peyton told me two weeks ago that whatever happened, he was at peace with it," Fulmer said. Then, Fulmer got in another shot at the outcome: "How they chose this is beyond me."

Asked if not winning the Heisman would change the way he viewed his college career, Manning said, "Absolutely not. ... It's not going to be a problem for me. I wouldn't change a thing about this past year or anything in my career. I wouldn't change one single thing. I did the best I could all year long, and that's all I ever wanted to do. I'll go home tonight and celebrate with my family and friends."

Celebrate? After not winning the Heisman?

The Mannings went to a Manhattan restaurant that night with friends from Tennessee, New Orleans and Mississippi.

"We had a big time," Archie Manning said. "When we got there, I told the group it's not going to be a morgue-type deal. It's a celebration. The whole night was a little disappointing, but I can't say it was totally unexpected. A lot of things were flying around about why this and why that. But like everything else, Peyton handled it well so there was no reason for everybody else not to handle it well.

"He wasn't pouting or sulking. He was ready to get away from there (Downtown Athletic Club) and not talk about it again."

Cutcliffe has a 5-by-7 framed photo in his office. It's a picture of Manning and Cutcliffe puffing on cigars at the restaurant. "That give you an indication of the mood?" Cutcliffe said. "We celebrated Peyton Manning. Everybody was letting some steam off, but it was not a gloomy evening."

Since that night, father and son have seldom talked about the Heisman Trophy. Cutcliffe and Manning talked about it on the flight from New York to Knoxville. "I think some of the regrets were the feeling of being set up, not so much the pain of not winning," Cutcliffe said. "I think he felt life is not always fair."

But what happened on Dec. 13 in New York did not detract from what Peyton Manning accomplished at Tennessee from 1994 to 1997. As Fulmer said: "We can celebrate that Peyton Manning is the best player in America."

Tennessee fans could also celebrate that Manning was third on the NCAA all-time list for passing yards, No. 4 for touchdown passes and first for career completion percentage and interception ratio.

If Manning was distraught about not winning the Heisman, it didn't deter his sense of humor. Heisman officials assign a limousine driver to each invited candidate. The morning after the Heisman ceremonies,

Archie Manning said the scrutiny placed on Peyton was unfair during the Heisman race. But that didn't stop the family from celebrating the night Peyton didn't win the Heisman.

Manning's driver asked Manning for an autograph. Manning told Cutcliffe he couldn't remember the driver's name.

"Hey," Cutcliffe said to the driver, "how do you spell your first name?"

The driver did a double-take, glared at Cutcliffe and said, "Bill, B-I-L-L."

Cutcliffe felt like a fool. "I swear," he said, "I think Peyton knew his name."

While Manning didn't lose his sense of humor, he felt the sting of not winning the Heisman. Archie Manning, who finished third in the Heisman voting in 1970 and fourth in 1969 while playing at Ole Miss, said he was disappointed because Peyton would have been a good ambassador for the Heisman.

"This happened for a reason and it wasn't meant to be," Archie said. "He ran a heck of a race. He just got caught up in the one year they (the media) made a big wave for a defensive player."

Long after Woodson had left the Downtown Athletic Club building and began celebrating on a freezing cold New York City night, Manning was still fielding a myriad of questions from the media - even though he wanted to dash out of there to join his family. Ten minutes became 20. Twenty became 30. Finally, 45 minutes later, the questions ended.

The long night was over for Manning. He walked slowly to see his family, which was stationed near the elevators on the 15th floor. He hugged his mother and father. His face was solemn. The Heisman wasn't his, but lasting respect was. He displayed class on a night when others might have been bitter, might have been angry, might have lashed out at a system that didn't seem fair.

Not Manning. Yes, he wanted to leave the premises earlier. But he didn't. He stayed because it was the right thing, the polite thing to do. He did the right thing when it came to accommodating the media his entire career. Some misguided folks even took shots at him for being a publicity hound, when he was merely being obliging. How could he win that debate? If he said yes to an interview request, he was seeking publicity. If he said no, he was a snob.

As Manning stood patiently, answering question after question, Cutcliffe peeked around the corner in admiration.

"He never ceases to amaze me," Cutcliffe said. "Watching him distinguish himself above the crowd, to see his response, to see how he handled it. He truly is above individual awards. It gave me more strength and belief in him.

"It shows the champion he really is. Everybody in Tennessee should celebrate that they've got a greater champion than they ever realized. Playing against a lot of good defenses in our league, and still throwing for more yards than anybody else that's played in the SEC, and to have played with a 1,000-yard rusher each of those years, that's distinguishing himself in a big way.

"It's a great statement for what Peyton has done. I think everybody deeply involved with college football knows what Peyton has done. And nobody in the country wouldn't trade their guy for Peyton Manning to start a program."

Probably not even Michigan's Carr. Carr was at Neyland Stadium on Nov. 29 to watch the Vols play Vanderbilt in the regular-season finale for both teams. Carr's son was a graduate assistant at Vanderbilt.

In the press box before the game, Carr was asked by a media member about the Heisman race. Carr said Woodson is a great player and valuable to the Michigan team, but Manning deserved the Heisman.

Yet, Woodson won it.

"Ask anybody who they wouldn't want to play against: Woodson or Manning," Cutcliffe said. "I'd take my chances with Woodson playing cornerback, receiver and returning punts as opposed to managing Peyton Manning for 70 snaps.

"Ask Joe Kines of Georgia if he'd rather see Charles Woodson at Tennessee and Manning at Michigan. He'd love to see Woodson at Tennessee and Manning at Michigan."

Ask former Arkansas defensive coordinator Joe Lee Dunn, whose Razorbacks were torched for 384 passing yards and 49 points by Manning in 1995. Ask defensive guru Bill "Brother" Oliver, whose Alabama defense gave up 301 passing yards and 41 points to Manning in 1996.

Chapter 8 – The "Heist-man" Trophy

Yet, Woodson won it.

The dye was cast the day before, when *USA Today* reported that
Woodson was ahead in five of the six regions. Even though the sampling
represented only 12 percent of the 921 voters, the projected outcome
wasn't close.

The survey proved accurate. Woodson received 433 first-place votes and
1,815 total points, based on a 3-2-1 point-system. Woodson won five
regions and was second in the sixth region.

Manning got 281 first-place votes and 1,543 points. Manning won the
South, but only by a 340-218 margin. He was second in the Southwest
and three other regions. He was third in the Far West.

Leaf was third with 70 first-place votes and 861 points.

An argument against Manning was that he didn't have impressive
numbers. Yet, Manning completed 287 of 477 passes (60.2 percent) for
3,816 yards and 36 touchdowns. He ranked among the nation's top
three in yards and TD passes. He threw only 11 interceptions. He led
Tennessee to an 11-1 record, a No. 3 ranking and its first SEC title in
seven years.

In 1996, Florida quarterback Danny Wuerffel won the Heisman.
Compared to Manning, Wuerffel had fewer passing yards, a lower
completion percentage, a higher interception ratio, and guided the
Gators to the same 11-1 record and No. 3 ranking entering the bowl
season.

Moreover, if statistics were a major factor, how would Woodson come
out on top? He had 43 tackles, seven interceptions, broke up five passes,
scored three touchdowns, caught 11 passes and averaged 8.6 yards per
punt return. By comparison, Tennessee had two cornerbacks with more
tackles, two defensive backs who broke up more than five passes, and
two punt returners who averaged more than 8.6 yards per return.

"I never knew what they were looking for," said Manning, who was
perplexed when he set a school record with 523 passing yards and five
touchdowns against Kentucky on Nov. 22, and lost ground in the
Scripps Howard Heisman poll to Woodson. That same day, Woodson
returned a punt for a touchdown and intercepted a pass in the end zone
against No. 4 Ohio State.

Manning talks to Florida quarterback Danny Wuerffel at the 1996 SEC
preseason media days conference. Wuerffel won the 1996 Heisman Trophy,
but Manning fell short in 1997 despite better numbers than Wuerffel.

Chapter 8 – The "Heist-man" Trophy

The Michigan-Ohio State game was on ABC nationally. The Tennessee-Kentucky game was played before a regional audience.

"I saw what was forming," Manning said. "I realized something was going on."

Cutcliffe was beside himself. "If Ohio State had been across the field from Peyton Manning that day, they would have been sorry, too," Cutcliffe said.

To counter Woodson's two-way player campaign, Cutcliffe said in November of that season, "Maybe we ought to let Peyton play some safety."

What many were looking for, it seemed, was a flaw, any flaw, as a reason not to vote for Manning. He didn't beat Florida. He didn't come up big in the biggest game. He had happy feet. He didn't throw the long ball well. He threw better to his right than his left.

Manning laughs at the last assertion. "I've always thought I threw better to my left because I got more (zip) on the ball," he said.

The year-long scrutiny of his son bothered Archie Manning. "It's not fair to do to a 21-year-old what they've done to him or what he's had to go through," Archie said. "I don't think anybody realizes. ... it's huge."

Archie wasn't happy with critics who, "Wanted to knock (Peyton) down," to build up Woodson.

"It's kind of what's going on in sports now," said Archie, a former color radio analyst for New Orleans Saints games. "At the pro level, some people are kind of brutal and it passes down to the college kids. That's the way it is. But, hey, he's a big boy. He knows what he's into."

A few weeks after ESPN carried the Heisman Trophy show, ESPN officials asked Archie if Peyton would attend an ESPY show in which Peyton was nominated as the college Player of the Year.

No thanks, Archie said.

But Peyton has a good chance to win, the ESPN official said.

No thanks.

OK, Peyton won, the spokesman finally said.

"We'll be there," Archie said.

Two months after the Heisman announcement, Manning again talked about the Heisman Trophy. He reiterated his disappointment for his family, fans and friends.

"For me personally, I was OK with it," he said. "Sure you want to win the best player of the year, whether it's Little League baseball or whatever. ... My life will be fine without it. I think it will make life a lot easier at least for the next few years."

No bitterness? No anger?

"If the reason I lost ... (pause) I didn't win was because a Southern quarterback won it the year before or they didn't want the front runner to win it, yes, that makes me mad, if they did that intentionally. Whether it's true or not, we'll never know."

The flak over the Heisman didn't go away soon in Knoxville or in the state of Tennessee. Fans bombarded the Downtown Athletic Club, ESPN and ABC with letters, mail and faxes, lambasting them for Manning not winning the Heisman.

They blamed ESPN and ABC, which owns ESPN, for conspiring to help Woodson win the Heisman because ABC carries Big Ten games. They complained that before all the votes were in Rudy Riska, executive director of the Heisman Memorial Trust, said it would be nice to see a defensive player win the award.

The animosity directed at ESPN might have been misguided. Nonetheless, ESPN "Game Day" anchor Chris Fowler, who spoke to the Knoxville Quarterback Club twice in recent years, called those who were blatant in their barbs "Tennessee Trailer Trash."

That led ESPN to release a statement that Fowler was not speaking for ESPN. A few days later, Fowler said his comment was aimed only at the UT fans who expressed vulgarity and went overboard in their objections.

That half-hearted apology didn't appease Tennessee fans. ESPN did a "Game Day" show from the Orange Bowl on Jan. 2, and guess who was playing in the Orange Bowl? Tennessee.

With the ESPN booth set up outside the stadium, Tennessee fans were unmerciful in taunting the ESPN crew of Fowler, Lee Corso and Kirk Herbstreit. Fowler later apologized to Bud Ford for his remarks. He also

Peyton Manning turned massive Neyland Stadium into Peyton's Place.
Tennessee averaged more than 106,000 per home game in Manning's last two
years, and played before the largest crowd in NCAA history against Florida in
1996.

Archie and Peyton Manning chat after a Tennessee practice. Archie was reluctant to talk to Peyton about the intricacies of playing quarterback, preferring to let Peyton's college coaches handle the specifics of the position.

Peyton has always looked up to Tennessee offensive coordinator David Cutcliffe, who believes the Colts will be a much better team with the rookie at quarterback. Cutcliffe said he slept well before Tennessee games, knowing Manning was at the helm.

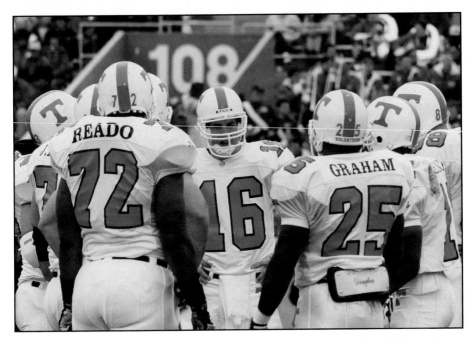

Peyton Manning didn't always have control of Tennessee's huddle. In Peyton's first game, offensive lineman Jason Layman told the talkative Manning ``shut the (bleep) up and call the play.''

Peyton Manning spent his first season at Tennessee handing off more than passing. He threw 144 passes as a true freshman, but at least 380 passes each of his last three seasons.

Though Manning's running ability was questioned, he proved to be elusive in the pocket. Manning had a 32-yard run against Virginia Tech in the 1994 Gator Bowl.

Wearing a necklace with broccoli, Manning stresses the importance of a proper diet as he reads to elementary children.

The students of Lotts Elementary School show their appreciation for a Peyton Manning appearance. Peyton did community service at schools, churches, and Boys and Girls Club, among others.

Manning signs yet another autograph at the Orange and White spring game and shares a laugh with teammate and roommate Trey Teague. One of the few disputes between Manning and Teague occurred during a ``Seinfeld" episode, when Manning had Teague practicing snaps.

Isidore Newman High School coach Frank Gendusa had plenty to smile about during Manning's three-year career. Gendusa and Manning were known to draw up plays in the dirt during games.

Eli Manning, like older brother Peyton, has college recruiters on their knees begging for his services. Eli's statistics as a sophomore and junior compare favorably with Peyton's numbers at the same stage of their careers.

Newman field was a happening place when the Mannings played at the Class AA school in New Orleans. The stadium seated 1,250, but crowds often exceeded 2,000 to watch Manning.

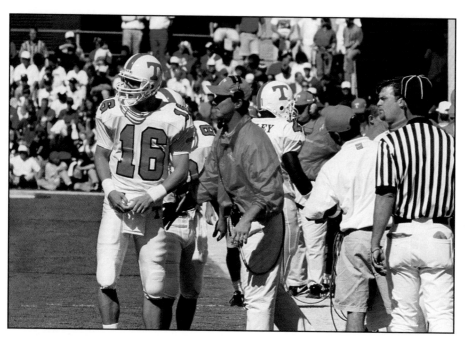

Peyton Manning didn't need much advice from Tennessee running backs coach and recruiting coordinator Randy Sanders. Manning became so efficient with Tennessee's offense, he rarely needed sideline assistance.

San Diego Chargers quarterbacks coach June Jones said Manning throws on the run as well as any young quarterback he's seen in a long time. Manning likely inherited that skill from his father, who was an excellent rollout passer in college and the NFL.

When Peyton was in uniform, his parents, Archie and Olivia, were usually at the stadium. Archie missed only one Tennessee game during Peyton's career. Olivia missed only a handful.

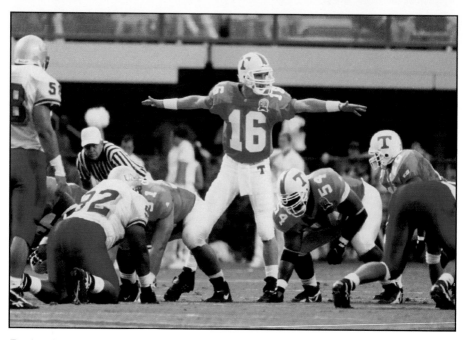

By the time Manning was a sophomore, he was directing traffic at the line of scrimmage.

Manning is driven through traffic in downtown Knoxville as the grand marshall of the Dogwood Arts Festival parade.

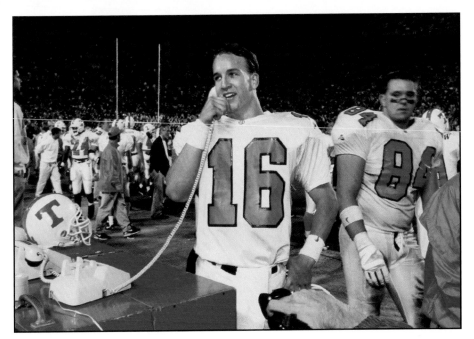

During the 1995 Alabama game, Manning laughed with Cutcliffe on the press box phone during a 41-14 blowout that snapped a nine-game winless streak against the Crimson Tide. Manning later scolded Cutcliffe for going conservative in the fourth quarter.

Manning was the consummate coach on the field, discussing a play with receiver Andy McCullough. Manning wasn't afraid to chew out teammates who dropped passes or didn't run proper routes.

Manning lets the referee know he scored a touchdown. Manning rushed for 12 touchdowns and threw for 89, accounting for a school record 101 scores at Tennessee. But his first college touchdown pass was nullified by an official (who was a family friend) because Manning was beyond the line of scrimmage when he threw the pass.

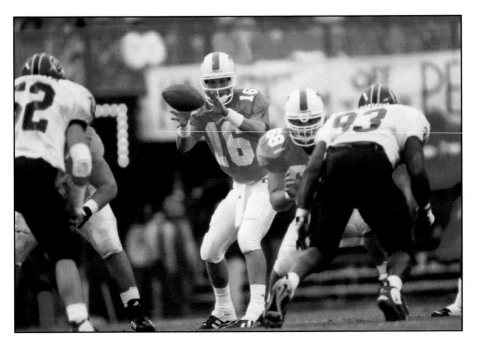

Although the shotgun formation wasn't Manning's forte, he used it effectively at times his last two years at Tennessee. Manning preferred taking the snap from under center because he was forced to take his eye off the defense to catch the shotgun snap.

In a pinch, Tennessee coach Phillip Fulmer wasn't afraid to put the outcome of games in the hands of Manning. Peyton had a 39-6 record at Tennessee, the most wins ever by a starter in the SEC.

Tennessee fans show their appreciation for Manning's decision to play his senior season at Tennessee.

Manning shakes hands with Smokey, Tennessee's mascot, as he makes his final run through the ``T'' formed by the band at Neyland Stadium.

Manning scores the game-winning touchdown on a bootleg against Vanderbilt in the last home game of his Tennessee career.

Peyton Manning became the first Tennessee athlete to win the prestigious James E. Sullivan Award as the nation's outstanding amateur athlete. Manning was only the fourth football player in the last 52 years to capture the honor.

Manning didn't get his hands on the coveted Heisman Trophy, finishing second to Michigan cornerback Charles Woodson. Eli, Cooper, Peyton, Olivia and Archie were all smiles before the disappointing announcement at New York's Downtown Athletic Club.

Manning received his degree in speech communication after just three years, earning a 3.6 grade-point average and winning the National Football Foundation and Hall of Fame scholar/athlete award. He is given his diploma by Lorayne Lester, dean of the college of arts and sciences.

Peyton hoists the plaque displaying his name on the jersey that was retired at Peyton Manning Appreciation Day on April 18, 1998. Manning was the first Vol to have his jersey retired.

NFL commissioner Paul Tagliabue helps Manning hold up the No. 18 jersey he will wear as an Indianapolis Colt.

Peyton Manning was intense during his first minicamp with the Indianapolis Colts in late April. Manning will wear No. 18 in the National Football League, the number his father wore during an All-American career at Ole Miss. Peyton and his brothers, Cooper and Eli, wore No. 18 in high school.

said he didn't think ESPN would do a "Game Day" show from Knoxville in 1998, because of the venom spewed forth by Vol fans. Knoxville has been a popular site for the ESPN "Game Day" over the last few years.

The message from Tennessee fans was clear, though sometimes too harsh. You can criticize our coach, our team, our program, but don't mess with our Manning.

Fowler said he voted for Manning, but he also defended Woodson.

"I emceed the Heisman dinner," Fowler said. "If people down there (the South) knew more about Charles Woodson the person, they wouldn't feel like it was a move away from class."

Tennessee fans found out more about Woodson, and they feel now more than ever the Heisman selection was a move away from class. At first, the UT fans' criticism of Woodson was that he was a showboat, a hot-dog. Woodson proclaimed himself the nation's best player in November. He struck the Heisman pose. He put the stem of a rose bush in his mouth after Michigan clinched a Rose Bowl berth. All of which left distaste in the mouths of Tennessee fans.

A sportswriter for a Detroit newspaper even referred to Woodson as, "a jerk."

At the NFL combine, Woodson was aloof.

Then came the Walter Camp Foundation banquet. It was held Feb. 14 in New Haven, Conn. Woodson, the Camp's Player of the Year, demanded a $5,000 appearance fee to accept the award. He also wanted first-class airline tickets for himself, his agent, his mother and his nephew. The cost: about $2,500.

The Walter Camp Foundation donates 100 percent of its net proceeds to children's charities. Woodson could have cared less. He wanted money to make the trip.

Walter Camp Foundation officials spent six hours on the phone with Woodson and/or his agent the day before the banquet. Finally, the morning of the banquet, Woodson agreed to come, but only if he got two first-class airline tickets, two coach tickets, plus hotel rooms for his traveling party, plus meals, plus free admission for his entourage to all Walter Camp events. The dinner alone costs $150 per plate. The cost to the Camp Foundation: about $3,500.

Woodson arrived at the Walter Camp children's banquet with two bodyguards. He refused to sign autographs. He refused interview requests from the Connecticut media.

"It's all about money," Walter Camp Foundation vice president Al Barbarotta said. "I wish we could re-vote for the Heisman Trophy and the Walter Camp Player of the Year. But we can't."

As for Manning, he showed up in Connecticut without bodyguards, signed autographs and held a press conference. He was, as usual, cordial and cooperative.

"You know, 99 percent of the athletes that come here are great," Barbarotta told the *Connecticut Post*. "They do all the hospital visits, sign all the autographs, they're just super. But that one percent, those are the people like Charles Woodson.

"It's terrible. I've been doing this for 18 years and Woodson is definitely one of the worst athletes we've ever had."

About a week later, Woodson, who was selected to the Maxwell All-American team, was a no show. Manning, who was the Maxwell Player of the Year, attended the banquet on Feb. 23. In winning the Maxwell, Manning became the first Tennessee football player to win a national award not limited by position.

On Feb. 25, Manning received the 68th annual Amateur Athletic Union Sullivan Award, given to the top amateur athlete in the nation based on character, leadership, athletic ability and the ideals of amateurism. Manning was the first University of Tennessee athlete to receive the honor. He was only the fourth football player to win the Sullivan and just the second in the past 52 years.

"Mr. Sullivan knew what playing sports is really all about," said Manning. "It's not about being the best. It's about discovering what your best is."

Manning thanked his teammates, his coaches and the entire University of Tennessee family.

"I know it will be nearly impossible for many people here at Tennessee to remember me as anything more than a football player," Manning

Manning won the prestigious Sullivan Award, given to the nation's top amateur athlete. Manning said he wanted to be remembered as more than just a football player at Tennessee.

said. "But in truth, I don't want to be remembered as a quarterback or No. 16. I hope that some day, I'll be remembered as a good person who happened to play football."

In some corners, the Sullivan Award is considered the nation's most prestigious amateur athlete award because it involves more than just football. But clearly the most recognized honor is the Heisman Trophy. And Manning didn't win it.

Manning was the prohibitive Heisman favorite when he announced in March of 1997 that he would return for his senior season at Tennessee. He probably would have been the No. 1 pick in the NFL draft had he turned pro after his junior season. Surely he was the top player in college football. He was even a Heisman favorite his junior year with his mug splashed upon countless football publications.

The Rocky Mountain News in Denver has conducted a weekly Heisman poll since 1986 for Scripps Howard news service. It consists of 10 voters, two each from five different regions of the United States. Each voter lists five candidates; the official Heisman ballot asks for three. The Scripps Howard poll represents about one percent of the Heisman's voters, so it is unscientific. But with one exception, its final poll had correctly forecast the Heisman winner.

Woodson wasn't among the 10 Heisman favorites entering the season. He didn't show up in the top five until October.

Manning lost support when Tennessee lost to Florida for the fifth year in a row. Manning was the starter for three of those games. While he didn't get much help from an offensive line that was overwhelmed by the Gators, Manning didn't play well, either. He threw a key first-quarter interception that was returned 89 yards for a touchdown by Tony George, setting the tone for the game.

Manning eventually passed for 353 yards - by far the highest passing total allowed by Florida last season - but much of his yardage came after the Gators had assumed a commanding lead. Florida was up 14-0 and 26-7 before winning 33-20.

After the game, Manning apologized to Tennessee fans for not playing well enough to help the Vols beat the hated Gators.

Sportswriter William Rhoden of the *New York Times* ripped Manning in a column the next day, proclaiming Manning was not a Heisman candidate because he could not win the big games. Rhoden later asserted that Woodson should win the Heisman because he is a better athlete than Manning, and that Woodson would make a better quarterback than Manning would make a cornerback. Misguided logic, but apparently shared by many.

Manning remained the front-runner for the Heisman, but his armor had a nick. It seemed many in the media were looking for someone else to vote for besides Manning. Running back Ricky Williams of Texas was having a great year, but his team wasn't. Running back Curtis Enis of Penn State was thrown into the race, but he didn't stick after the Nittany Lions lost to Michigan.

Moss might have been the best talent in the nation, but he played at tiny Marshall, which played a weak schedule. Plus, he had a criminal record and an attitude.

Leaf was having a great season for a Washington State team that would finish the regular season 10-1. But he didn't have enough support to bypass a more heralded player at the same position.

That left Woodson, an extraordinary cornerback who played just enough offense to be hailed as a two-way player. He had 78 snaps on offense and caught 11 passes. He also returned punts. Although he didn't rank among the nation's top 60 in punt returns, he had a touchdown runback against Ohio State in a huge game.

That sealed the deal for Woodson, even though he was no more versatile than two players from Georgia: Hines Ward and Champ Bailey. Woodson just happened to play on the nation's No. 1 team.

A Michigan publicist said Woodson accounted for three touchdowns during the Wolverines 20-14 victory over Ohio State. He returned a punt for a touchdown, and he intercepted a pass in the end zone to thwart an Ohio State drive.

The third TD? Well, he said, another Wolverine intercepted a pass and returned it for a touchdown, but Woodson deserves credit because the Buckeyes wouldn't throw Woodson's way.

Critics said Woodson was given way too much credit for

intangibles while Manning wasn't given enough. Manning made his teammates better, he was clutch in the fourth quarter, he managed a game brilliantly - only twice his senior season did he call the wrong pass protection and get sacked - and he was excellent in the two-minute offense.

All that didn't matter.

In a year when Heisman voters were looking for another candidate to challenge the favorite, looking to honor a defensive player and a versatile athlete, they found one in Woodson. The snowball stopped on the doorsteps of the Downtown Athletic Club.

Rudy Riska, executive director of the Heisman Memorial Trust in New York City for the past 37 years, found himself in hot water during the process. He was quoted in *USA Today* as saying "it would be good, not only for the Heisman Trophy, but college football" if a defensive player won the award. Because Woodson was the only defensive player in contention, Riska's remark was perceived by some as an endorsement of Woodson.

Riska denied endorsing Woodson.

"I said it would be good for college football (if a defensive player won) because it would give other position players the feeling they would not be excluded over a running back or a quarterback," Riska said. "I've been here for 37 years and I wouldn't select anyone. I'm as impartial as could be.

"It came out like I said, 'Woodson (should win it).' I never even mentioned Woodson's name. That doesn't mean I would say Peyton Manning wouldn't have the opportunity to win it."

Riska said he apologized to Archie Manning and Bud Ford before the Heisman voting was announced. Manning and Ford might have accepted the apology, but they bristled at what Riska had done.

Riska said the Downtown Athletic Club received about 300 letters and faxes from irate Tennessee fans within a week of the Heisman announcement. Some were vulgar, some were rational.

"We can understand their feelings," Riska said. "But I resent some of the crazzos."

The Downtown Athletic Club received one fax with a Dr. (Jack) Kevorkian certificate, saying the doctor would assist in any suicide attempts.

 Riska didn't endear himself to the Mannings or Tennessee fans when he added: "I still believe it will be good for college football (that a defensive player won the award). For 63 years, we got criticized because the award didn't go to a defensive player. Now, we're criticized for a defensive player winning the award."

In the Manning camp, older brother Cooper was philosophical:

"I think Peyton deserved the Heisman," Cooper Manning said. "I'm not sure the Heisman deserved Peyton."

Endless hours of film room study allowed Peyton Manning to make quick decisions on the run.

Chapter Nine:

The Legacy

"I'll be fortunate if I ever come across another athlete who is the total package like Peyton"

– Mike Rollo
Tennessee trainer

IN DECEMBER OF 1994, JOE HARRINGTON, TENNESSEE'S visual resource specialist for football, was given a Christmas present by an innocent-looking freshman quarterback named Peyton Manning.

"This is kind of odd," Harrington said, opening a package that contained a golf shirt. "I've never had a player give me a Christmas present before. I thought: What is the deal here?"

Harrington found out what the deal was. The gift wasn't for what Harrington had done for Manning, but for what Manning expected Harrington to do.

When Manning was a freshman, he studied film. He watched every practice. During two-a-days, he'd watch the morning workout before he'd eat lunch, then watch it a second time with the coaches before the afternoon drills. He'd watch himself, second guess his decisions, make sure he knew the defensive coverages.

As a sophomore, Manning became a fanatic. Or maybe, an addict. He had to watch football film. Every day. He had to study. Every day. He had to know what was going on. He was obsessed. The deal was, Harrrington discovered, Manning wanted favors.

"He asked me for a ton of tapes," Harrington said.

And with the frequent visits to Harrington, Manning would throw in a reminder about that golf shirt he bought Harrington: "You get a chance to wear that shirt? How's it fit?"

Then came: "By the way, can I have this and this and this?"

At the end of a football season, Manning's Expedition was filled with three or four large garbage bags of tapes.

"All of them were watched and none of them were rewound," Harrington said. "I don't know if it was because he was lazy or to prove to me he'd watched them all. Or his VCR didn't have a rewind feature."

Harrington estimated he prepared for Manning 15 tapes a week during a 13-week season. That's almost 200 tapes. And Manning would watch them all. Every one of them.

Manning had each Tennessee opponent's schedule memorized. If Harrrington tried to take any short cuts, or didn't have that revealing Vanderbilt-Northern Illinois tape, Manning would notice. "He didn't want any surprises," Harrington said.

Peyton is fond of a quote given to him by his father that came from former Pittsburgh Steelers coach Chuck Noll: "Pressure is something you feel when you don't know what the hell you're doing."

Said Manning: "I'm not going to feel pressure because I'm going to watch enough film and know what I'm doing back there."

Not all of his film sessions were productive. One Sunday, Manning was watching tape in the team room. Harrington walked by. He glanced inside. The tape rewound itself about 20 times.

"I walked in the room and Peyton had fallen asleep with the remote in his hand," Harrington said.

Peyton could get a little pushy. He wanted Harrington to make cutups of only his practice repetitions so Manning wouldn't be slowed by watching the other quarterbacks. "Remember the golf shirt," Manning would say. That's one favor Manning couldn't wiggle out of Harrington.

A few days after being drafted by the Indianapolis Colts, Manning the film buff, already was creating headaches for Marty Hetcher, the Colts' head video coordinator. Manning was hounding Hetcher for practice tapes. The Colts, like many other NFL teams, use Beta tapes for better quality. Manning has a VHS video cassette recorder. The two are not

Manning laughs with Joe Harrington, Tennessee visual resource specialist for football, at a Tennessee practice in the spring of 1998. Peyton bribed Harrington with gifts in exchange for practice and game tapes.

compatible.

Hetcher told Manning to buy a Beta machine, which costs $18,000. Manning said his $100 VCR worked just fine and he wanted Hetcher to convert the Beta tapes to VHS tapes, a time-consuming process. Hetcher said the Colts were on the verge of paying Peyton a $10 million signing bonus, so Manning could afford a Beta machine.

One legacy Manning leaves at Tennessee is his dedication to film watching. He is the master of the remote. But there's a reason for it. Peyton does nothing, unless there is a reason. He watches film as a means to compete as a quarterback.

"One of Peyton's greatest assets is, he's a fierce competitor," said Tennessee offensive coordinator David Cutcliffe. "He's constantly competing to be the best he can be."

Manning was asked if he is a better quarterback or competitor.

"I like to think I'm a quarterback who loves to compete," Manning said. "You see guys playing quarterback and they just say, 'I'm not sure what's going on with this defense, but I can get it done because I can compete.' I'm not one of those. I like to prepare for them and know exactly what's going on, and when the time comes to compete, then compete."

His legacy is not confined to competition. He leaves a legacy of leadership, of being the first Tennessee athlete to have his jersey - not his number - retired. He had a street named after him: Peyton Manning Pass. It is near Neyland Stadium, where the players make "The Walk" on game days. Babies are named after him. He spent hundreds of hours doing community service. He studied Tennessee football history, and so respected its former players, he attended the recent funerals of John "Skeeter" Bailey and George Cafego. He was Tennessee's first All-American quarterback since Bobby Dodd in 1930. He won more games than any quarterback in Southeastern Conference history. And he set 33 Tennessee records.

Peyton Manning became the most popular athlete in Tennessee history.

Entering his sophomore year, Manning found his mug on just about every cover of a preseason football magazine. *Lindy's* even made

Even while in the grasp of a defender, Manning continued to compete. "He's a fierce competitor," Cutcliffe said.

Manning stands underneath the street sign bearing his name with girlfriend Ashley Thompson. Manning led the Vols on "The Walk" to the stadium about two hours before home games.

Manning their first-team All-American quarterback. And the guy hadn't even played an entire game by himself, having shared time as a freshman with Branndon Stewart.

"I finally had to buy *Playgirl* to find a magazine that didn't have his picture on it," Cooper Manning said.

Manning made the cover of more magazines than any other Tennessee athlete in history. He did numerous public service announcements. He was on Tennessee's media guide cover, on posters, on calendars. No wonder Neyland Stadium came to be known as Peyton's Place.

The depth of his notoriety landed him on CBS' "This Morning" news. He became the first college athlete to be a guest on David Letterman's late-night talk show. Manning's appearance on Dec. 8, 1997, did Tennessee proud.

Like everything else he does, Manning prepared for the show as he and Cooper did a background check on Letterman. Letterman asked about Peyton's decision to return for his final season at Tennessee

Manning: "I wanted to come back and enjoy my senior year - just like your great senior year at Ball State."

Lettermen then asked Manning about his knee injury suffered in the SEC championship game the week before.

Manning: "As a matter of fact, I went to the doctor's office today - it was the same doctor you went to eight years ago for your knee, I think."

Letterman, stunned: "The kid's got writers."

Manning wasn't above a friendly bribe.

As a sophomore in high school, Manning bought his offensive lineman those Isotoner gloves peddled by Dan Marino. The next year, he bought them Gatorade T-shirts. As a freshman at Tennessee, Manning bought chicken wings for his blockers. Later, he bought them dress shirts, probably to replace the ones that needed laundering from spilled chicken wings.

"I take care of them at the end of the year," Manning said. "It's kind of an official quarterback/lineman deal."

Peyton Manning: Primed and Ready

It's Manning-the-quarterback's way of showing he appreciates the protection he gets from his offensive linemen. Apparently it works. Manning's senior season at Tennessee, the Vols set a school record for fewest sacks allowed per pass attempt.

"You have to have some sort of relationship for those guys to protect you and want to lay it on the line for you," said Manning, who roomed with two different offensive lineman — Will Newman, then Trey Teague — and was a host for several other offensive linemen on their official visits to Tennessee.

When Manning was a senior, he sat next to freshman offensive lineman Cosey Coleman on the bus ride to the Kentucky game, just to get acquainted.

At Tennessee's training table, Manning went from table to table like a politician. He ate with running backs one meal, receivers the next. He sat with offensive linemen, defensive linemen. He broke bread with linebackers and defensive backs, kickers and punters.

If he saw a player sitting by himself, he paid a visit. It was his way of showing leadership, his way of making sure the team wasn't polarized. His thoughtfulness carried into the public eye. In September of 1997, when Tennessee students formed a long line to pick up tickets for an upcoming Florida game, Manning treated the faithful with boxes of pizza.

"Networking," Tennessee trainer Mike Rollo called it. "He always moved around. That's why he was so popular with the team. He worked at not just being a quarterback, but connecting with the team. Peyton tried to be close with everybody."

That's why Manning could post a note on a door at Tennessee's indoor complex calling for "mandatory" summer workouts with the receivers, and get a strong response. It's illegal to have mandatory workouts during the summer, so Manning put up another note asking teammates to "please come" to the "voluntary" workouts.

If someone didn't show for a day or two, then dropped a pass during the drills, Manning would let him hear about it. When six players missed one of the workouts, Manning listed their names on the next "workout notice" and put an asterisk by Jay Graham's name. The asterisk stood for team captain.

"I was just ragging him a bit," Manning said.

Manning could get away with it, because no one worked harder, no one paid a greater price, no one wanted to win more.

His pain threshold was remarkable. He suffered a painful second-degree sprained medial collateral ligament against Arkansas in 1996, quickly had his knee taped, and didn't miss a snap. He missed just one practice. In fact, in four seasons at Tennessee, Manning missed just one practice - not counting the Orange Bowl workouts his senior season.

When Manning ruptured the bursa sac in his right knee during the Dec. 6 SEC Championship game against Auburn, it became infected. Manning could hardly walk for days. But, according to Rollo, he did a "miraculous job" just to play in the Orange Bowl.

"Peyton is a person who doesn't complain about pain," Rollo said. "Other athletes, that's all they think about is pain. I've never seen Peyton overcome by pain."

When Manning arrived at Tennessee he felt it was important to learn about his new school's football history. "I've always felt like if you play at a place like this, if you don't appreciate the people who played here before you, you're doing it the wrong way," Manning said.

Manning read a book on former Tennessee coach Gen. Robert Neyland, one of college football's all-time great coaches. He asked Tennessee officials questions about former players, former coaches, interesting contests. He gobbled up tapes of old games.

One of the first tapes he watched was Tennessee v. Ole Miss in 1968. Archie Manning threw six interceptions as the Rebels lost 31-0. Peyton sent a note to his father: "Dad, you were terrible,"

In 1969, Ole Miss got revenge, winning 38-0. Note from Peyton to Archie: "You redeemed yourself."

Tennessee publicist Haywood Harris was telling Manning about a Tennessee-UCLA game in 1965. "That's the one where they had the fight," Manning said.

Harris was stunned. "What impressed me was Peyton knew so much about Tennessee football history that he knew about an individual game that happened 32 years ago," Harris said.

As a graduate student in the fall of 1997, Manning took an independent study class under Tennessee professor Andy Kozar, a former Tennessee star fullback and a history buff. To help with Dr. Kozar's research project on Neyland, Manning interviewed former Vol greats George Cafego and Doug Atkins. Atkins is from Humboldt, Tenn., hometown of Peyton's fraternal grandmother, Sis Manning.

Manning said he would loved to have met Neyland, who died in 1962. "Former players said his discipline helped them in life," said Manning. "I consider myself to be a disciplined guy. People tell me I would have enjoyed playing for him."

Manning etched his name beside Atkins and Cafego and Dodd and Reggie White as one of Tennessee's all-time greats. He is the fourth Vol to finish runner-up for the Heisman Trophy. He set an SEC record for career passing yards. He set 33 school records, including most touchdown passes, most pass completions and attempts, most total yards and most 300-yard passing games. He set seven SEC records and two NCAA records.

Manning's career was so brilliant, Tennessee honored him by retiring his jersey - No. 16 with Manning written across the back - at the spring game in April 1997. It was the same day he was the No. 1 pick in the National Football League draft.

"We think this is the appropriate step to recognize and honor one of our great athletes," Tennessee athletic director Doug Dickey said.

Yet, according to many fans, that wasn't enough. They thought Manning's number should have been retired. The Manning family said they were "excited" and "flattered" that Peyton's jersey was retired, but privately they felt that retiring a jersey was a bit watered down.

"I didn't want to get our feet in that creek because if you do, you'd have to do it year after year," said UT president Dr. Joe Johnson. Dewey Warren, a former star quarterback at Tennessee who also wore No. 16, was critical. He said Manning's number should have been retired.

"Who has been a greater ambassador for the university over the last four years?" Warren asked. "Who has brought more notoriety? Who has handled it by being a humble kid? Who graduated in three years with a

Manning gets a hug from his father as Tennessee retired Peyton's jersey at the 1998 spring game.

3.6 (grade-point average)? What other athlete has done as much for the university as Peyton Manning?

"I was the first Tennessee quarterback to wear No. 16. It would be great to see Peyton be the last."

Dickey pointed out that the University of Kentucky in basketball and the Dallas Cowboys, among others, retire jerseys, not numbers. Four former Tennessee players killed in World War II had their numbers retired. Otherwise, Dickey said Tennessee has a policy not to retire numbers.

"If you start getting into former players who have earned recognition," Dickey said, "you start depleting your numbers to where it gets uncomfortable. ... We've tried to be fair and considerate of all of our heroes."

But Tennessee did not call former players to see if they would be offended if Manning's number were retired. Condredge Holloway, Hank Lauricella, Heath Shuler, Kozar and Warren, among others, said they were not contacted and, no, they would not have been offended. Johnny Majors also was not contacted, but said a Tennessee policy about retiring numbers is, "beyond my interest and concern."

Nonetheless, if Manning's number were retired, Tennessee would have to strongly consider retiring the numbers of Doug Atkins, Beattie Feathers, Bob Suffridge, Majors, White and Cafego, among others.

Tennessee established a Peyton Manning Scholarship Fund. Manning brought in some $166,500 in scholarship money from various entities, including $100,000 for winning the Burger King/Vincent dePaul Draddy Award, which goes to the National Football Foundation and College Hall of Fame national scholar-athlete of the year. Proceeds from the 1998 spring football game and from individual donors raised thousands more for the fund.

Manning also has $28,000 in post-graduate scholarship money he can use if he chooses to pursue his education. He graduated cum laude with the highest grade-point average in his major, speech communication. Education was always important to Manning. His parents said they never had to tell him to do his homework.

"Peyton has the brains of a lawyer, the heart of a warrior and the soul of a gentleman," said Carmen Tegano, an associate athletic director at Tennessee who is in charge of academic counseling. "I won't see another kid like him. I hope I do, but I know I won't."

But he's not perfect. There was the mooning incident. And he admits he's been late for class. And "my girlfriend yells at me."

Said Cooper: "Peyton has a pretty good record. Most of the things he did bad, they blamed on me."

No SEC quarterback won as many games as a starter — not Joe Namath, not Ken Stabler, not Pat Sullivan, not Bert Jones, not Babe Parilli, not Danny Wuerffel, not Archie Manning. Peyton's record was 39-6. He was the first quarterback in SEC history to beat Alabama three times. He is No. 3 on the NCAA's all-time chart for passing yards (11,201) and No. 4 for touchdown passes (89).

For all Manning did for Tennessee, football coach Phillip Fulmer asks: "How are we going to manage without him?"

"I feel I'm really blessed to have played with a quarterback as good as Peyton Manning," said Vols receiver Andy McCullough. Tennessee receiver Peerless Price said he would brag to his grandchildren that he played with Manning. Baldwin Montgomery, Manning's teammate at Newman High School, has the utmost respect for Manning. "He really is a role model," Montgomery said. "I'd love my kids to grow up like him."

Kids admire him.

Adults admire him.

"In today's world, you see a lot of people saying they're not role models, that they don't want to accept that responsibility," Manning said. "I disagree. In my four years at Tennessee, I tried to be a person the people could look up to. I'm not doing it for any fake reasons. That's the person I want to be. My parents taught me to do the right thing and that's what I try to do. It's pretty simple advice."

An editorial in the *Indianapolis Star* said: "It sure appears that Archie and Olivia Manning did a pretty good job of raising their boy, Peyton. So we're optimistic that Manning will be a great addition to the Colts roster."

Tennessee's director of Student Life Carmen Tegano, flanked by Peyton and Archie, said: "I won't see another kid like Peyton."

Chapter 9 – The Legacy

A few years ago, Trey Teague vacationed with Manning in Cancun, Mexico. Teague couldn't believe the attention Manning received. He shook his head when he thought about the adulation in and out of the United States.

"You have grown men that idolize him and that's kind of sickening to some of us," Teague said. "It's great to be a fan and great for the kids. But sometimes it gets out of hand.

"Some people need to get their priorities in line. When you're six years old, that's natural. When you're 50 and come in dressed head to toe in orange and about to pass out (because you're going to get Manning's autograph), come on."

Manning displayed his typical humility during the Cancun trip. Manning and some other football players arrived at the All-Star Café, only to learn the wait would be two hours. Manning went to the back of the line. His party urged him to use his influence so the manager would let them in sooner. Manning refused.

Finally, the other players dragged Manning toward the front of the line where the manager recognized him, ushered them inside and had him sign, oh, about a million items.

Tim Layden, a senior writer for *Sports Illustrated*, spent a week with Manning during Manning's sophomore season, even going to class with the quarterback. Layden spent more time with Manning the next spring and fall, and built a close relationship with Manning and the Manning family.

"I honestly think Peyton is one of the most mature, interesting college athletes I've ever met," Layden said. "He has a genuine sense of humor and joy that he fights to keep quiet in public. The best of him is when he lets his guard down around people he knows, family and friends. It's a shame Tennessee people didn't get to see what a fun, vibrant person he could be. I like him as much as anyone I've dealt with.

"I think he handled what he was dealt at Tennessee very well."

What he was dealt was inordinate adoration. A giraffe at the Knoxville Zoo was named after Peyton. More than 100 new-born babies in East Tennessee were named after Peyton.

Peyton Manning: Primed and Ready

"That's crazy," Olivia Manning said. "I think it's a wonderful name, I do. And I think it's wonderful to be honored that way. But it's a little overwhelming. It's pretty amazing."

In college, Archie had dogs and cats and horses named after him.

"I guess Peyton's bumped up to human status, which, I guess, is a plus," Cooper Manning said.

Manning's popularity bumped him to legendary status.

"Peyton Manning is definitely a legend around here," Rollo said. "He is one of those once-in-a-lifetime athletes, not just as a football player, but as a person. He's unique. You can't do all the things he did in college. He wants to get the job done. He wants to help people. He wants to please people.

"If you're defining a person of incredible character and personality, I think you can define him with just the name Peyton Manning. He is a class act. I'll be fortunate if I ever come across another athlete who is the total package like Peyton. The athlete, the player, the person, the character, the student, the image, the community service. All those things don't come together at one point very often. I don't know if we'll ever see another one."

The Knoxville Zoo thought Manning was so special it named a baby giraffe after the Tennessee quarterback. Peyton had at least 100 children named after him.

Peyton Manning got his wish by being the No. 1 overall selection in the 1998 draft, going to the Indianapolis Colts.

Chapter Ten:

Colts Finally Get Their Elway

"My career at Tennessee has been special. I hope to have a better career at Indianapolis."

– Peyton Manning

PEYTON MANNING DIDN'T WANT TO GO TO NEW YORK for the NFL draft April 18. He'd been there four months earlier for the Heisman Trophy ceremonies. We know how that turned out.

"I don't like these things where I have to wait for somebody to announce what's going to happen," Manning said. "I haven't done too well with those things in the past."

No, Peyton Manning wasn't going to New York. Unless.

Unless he *knew* he would be the Indianapolis Colts' No. 1 pick, the top overall selection in the NFL draft. He had to know he wouldn't be upstaged by Washington State quarterback Ryan Leaf.

Maybe he did. He says he didn't.

He went anyway. Because the league asked him to. "No point in starting off on bad terms, I guess," he said.

But surely he had an inkling. He must have known something when Colts owner Jim Irsay invited him - not Leaf - for breakfast at the Surf Club in Miami Beach in early April. As he departed, Manning looked Irsay in the eyes and said: "I'll win for you."

Those words made a huge impact on Irsay.

"They sent shivers down my spine," Irsay said. "I knew then he was the guy I wanted."

The meeting reinforced Irsay's perception of Manning.

"It's kind of like (the movie) 'Titanic,'" Irsay told the *Indianapolis Star*. "You hear how good it is, but until you experience it for yourself, you don't really know. I think it would be impossible for anyone to present himself any better than he does. I don't know if in the last 25 years a guy has come out (of college) this mature and with such a balance of confidence and humility. I was very impressed."

From that point, it was widely speculated that Irsay would take Manning over Leaf. But it wasn't official. Indianapolis waited until draft day to break the news.

This was an extremely important pick for the Colts. They had come oh-so-close to having an unbelievable run of quarterbacks over the past 40 years, from Johnny Unitas to Bert Jones to John Elway. Instead, they had Unitas, followed closely by Jones. The Colts drafted Elway, a star at Stanford, but he refused to sign. Elway, a second-round pick of the New York Yankess in 1981, threatened to pursue a professional baseball career, thus forcing a trade that would keep him near his home, the West Coast.

The date that lives in infamy for the Colts: May 2, 1983. That's when the Colts traded Elway to Denver for offensive lineman Chris Hinton, quarterback Mark Herrmann and Denver's second-round pick in the 1984 draft, which turned out to be lineman Ron Stolt.

Tracing the trade, the only remaining remnant for Indianapolis is receiver Marvin Harrison.

Since shipping Elway out West, the Colts have had 16 different starting quarterbacks: Herrmann, Art Schlichter, Gary Hogeboom, Mike Pagel, Matt Kofler, Jack Trudeau, Blair Kiel, Chris Chandler, Tom Ramsey, Jeff George, Don Majkowski, Browning Nagle, Craig Erickson, Jim Harbaugh, Kelly Holcomb and Paul Justin.

Moreover, while Elway was taking Denver to four Super Bowls and winning more games (138) than any quarterback in NFL history, the Colts were having five winning seasons and making two playoff appearances in 15 years.

Chapter 10 – Colts Finally Get Their Elway

So the Colts couldn't afford to screw up this pick.

"I want to make the pick personally to make a symbolic gesture to put the ghost of Elway to rest," Irsay said, later adding: "We have to win a championship before you can put all the ghosts to rest."

On April 18, 1998, the Colts made Peyton Manning the No. 1 overall pick in the NFL. Manning became the ninth quarterback since 1970 to be the first player selected. Of the other eight, five went to a Super Bowl and four have combined to win 10 Super Bowls. Elway won one, in 1998. The ghost won't go away.

Manning or Leaf. Leaf or Manning. It really didn't matter. The Colts couldn't go wrong with either. Or could they?

"It doesn't really matter which one we get," said San Diego Chargers general manager Bobby Beathard, whose team traded up from the third slot to get the second overall pick.

Experts said the same thing about Drew Bledsoe and Rick Mirer, who were the first two picks of the 1993 draft. Bledsoe, like Leaf, left Washington State a year early to turn pro. Mirer, like Manning, stayed in college to play his senior season, at Notre Dame.

Bledsoe took New England to the Super Bowl in 1996 and made All-Pro. Mirer, who had a promising rookie season, played his way out of Seattle and rode Chicago's bench in 1997.

Jerry Angelo, director of player personnel for Tampa Bay, told *Sports Illustrated:* "Quarterback is the toughest position in sports to coach, to evaluate and to play. A few years ago, we studied the top 30 quarterbacks of all time. The No. 1 trait we found was toughness; they all had it. No. 2 was accuracy. No. 3 was instincts. The last was work ethic and maturity. Peyton's got them all. He's talented and he'll handle the inferno of going to a 3-13 team. He's a sure player ... as sure as you can be about anybody in this league."

With no guarantees, the Colts diligently did their homework. They were the only team out of 30 not to clear Manning's inflamed right knee - he was hurt in a game on Dec. 6, 1997 - at the NFL Combine in February. He made a special trip to Indianapolis in early April to get cleared.

Peyton Manning and Ryan Leaf applaud after Michigan's Charles Woodson is announced the 1997 Heisman Trophy winner. Manning and Leaf got acquainted during the Heisman ceremonies in New York. Leaf thought Manning should have won the Heisman. Leaf also thought Manning should have been the No. 1 overall pick in the NFL draft.

The Colts made a special trip to Knoxville to work out Manning on April 1. President and general manager Bill Polian, head coach Jim Mora, offensive coordinator Tom Moore and quarterbacks coach Bruce Arians sent Manning through a closed, 45-minute workout.

It was a strange workout. Manning threw primarily to stationary targets. "Old-man routes," Manning called them. Manning felt he threw the ball well. Asked what the Colts were looking for, Manning said: "I don't know, they didn't really say."

Interestingly, June Jones, the new quarterbacks coach of the San Diego Chargers, asked for and received permission to observe Manning during the April 1 session. Afterwards, Colts officials weren't talking. They hopped on Irsay's private jet and flew to Pullman, Wash., to test Leaf.

Jones wasn't in such a rush. And he talked. "Having the background with his dad and being around the Saints when he was growing up, he's as advanced mentally as I've seen coming out," said Jones, who felt Manning was more prepared to play immediately in the NFL than Leaf.

"Manning has played more football and thrown more passes. He's been in a very tough conference and played big-time college football. Ryan has had a great run this year at Washington State, but he hasn't played as much as Peyton. He (Manning) is going to be a great player. He's got all the tools."

The tools. Everyone got into comparing the tools of Manning and Leaf. There wasn't much difference in size. Manning is 6 feet 5 inches and 230 pounds. Leaf is 6 feet 5-and-a-half inches and weighs 240. Leaf has a stronger arm, but Manning's arm is strong enough. Manning has the quicker release, is more accurate, has better touch, and surveys the field better. Leaf is considered more athletic and stronger.

Manning got the edge in intangibles, leadership and experience. Manning started 45 games in four years at Tennessee. Leaf made 23 starts in two years at Washington State. Experts said one concern about Manning was his decision-making against quick, pass rushing teams like Florida. The Colts line gave up an American Football Conference-high and team-record 62 sacks last year.

Both quarterbacks' mobility is similar, but Leaf is harder to tackle. Yet, Jones said of Manning: "I think he throws on the move as well as any young guy I've seen in a while." When Manning's mobility was compared to Bernie Kosar, Manning objected: "I think I'm a little quicker than Bernie. I always felt when it was time to get away, I've been able to get away."

A sampling of what NFL personnel said:

Tom Braatz, Miami Dolphins scouting director: "One of them (Leaf) has a chance to fail. The other one (Manning) has no chance to fail."

Glenn Cumbee, Tennessee Oilers scouting director: "Peyton may have been undersold at times this year. He's been the standard by which others are judged. He's a very cerebral player who will do everything in the film room. He's prepared, executes all types of throws, plays well in pressure. He has the whole list."

Mike Brown, Cincinnati Bengals general manager: "Manning's arm is strong enough. He's bright. He's quick in his decision-making. I'm not saying he'll be the next Elway, but if I have to guess, Manning will develop into a top NFL quarterback."

Former San Francisco 49ers coach Bill Walsh: "I don't see (Brett) Favre or Elway. But Manning seems to be more pro-ready than Leaf."

Sid Gillman, a long-time NFL head coach and offensive innovator: "Now this (Manning) is a pro quarterback. I'd draft this kid in a second."

Denver Broncos coach Mike Shanahan: "Peyton will make every throw there is."

Former New York Giants Super Bowl quarterback Phil Simms: "In the NFL, you make your living throwing the intermediate pass, and look at how many good intermediate throws Peyton makes."

Com Anile, Carolina Panthers scouting director: "Manning is super intelligent. He's going to be able to help you right away."

Perhaps Anile's assessment, as much as anything, triggered the Colts to pick Manning No. 1. As Polian said after the draft: "It would have been much harder for me to explain why we took someone else."

Even Leaf said he would have selected Manning first. "He's the smart thing to do," Leaf said. "What else does he have to prove? I still have a lot of things to prove to people. If you're going to risk your franchise and the No. 1 pick in the draft, you want to be really secure about it."

The Colts weren't so secure about Leaf. He reported to the NFL combine at a robust 261 pounds. It raised some eyebrows. On one of the biggest days of Leaf's life, when you're exposing yourself to your future employer, Leaf exposed a big belly, compliments of the banquet circuit.

Then, Leaf missed a meeting with Mora, who values promptness as much as paychecks. Instead, Leaf had a physical examination scheduled with another team. Leaf and Mora exchanged barbs in the media. Mora called Leaf irresponsible.

"I think that Coach Mora acting the way he did by being so public was a ploy," Leaf said. "He wants Peyton, so by making a big deal out of what was a simple misunderstanding, he could go back to the Colts organization and say: 'See, he missed an appointment. He's irresponsible. That's why we need to draft Peyton.' He tried to humiliate me for his own selfish reasons.

"The whole thing was terrible. It made me very uncomfortable. It made me think: 'Why should I play for this team? If this is how they do business, why would I want to go there?' If I go to Indy, hopefully we can work through all of this bitterness. I'm willing to. But frankly, I don't think they are going to draft me. And I'd rather play on the West Coast."

Manning had a preference for the South.

"Growing up around the South for 22 years, it'd be nice to play in this area," Manning said on Feb. 25. "But it's really not a high priority. I'm prepared for all climates and for turf or grass.

"All I want to do is get to an organization that can win some games. I know the Colts have a great organization. Getting Jim Mora is a real plus. And Bill Polian is one of the best general managers around."

Leaf feared the Leaf-Manning comparisons would create a rift between the two. Leaf called Manning and they quickly became friends. They spent time together in New York the night before the draft on an NFL-sponsored cruise boat outing. Leaf had an entourage of about 30, and most of them asked Manning for an autograph. Some asked Manning to sign "Official Heisman Trophy" footballs.

"I'm not real fond of those," Manning said, referring to his negative experience during the Heisman ceremonies in December at the Downtown Athletic Club. It's still a sore subject for the family.

"That time here was miserable," Olivia Manning said. "Peyton's knee was a mess. Things didn't go very well. ... I know this, we won't be riding by the Downtown Athletic Club."

Polian used the No. 1 pick as a carrot. He dangled it in front of his former employers, the Carolina Panthers, who were willing to trade young quarterback Kerry Collins, draft picks and proven players for the right to select Manning. The deal didn't materialize, however.

Peyton Manning sings with friends at a Knoxville restaurant the night after he was the NFL's No. 1 draft choice and had his jersey retired by Tennessee. Zane Daniels (holding microphone), Cooper Manning and Teddy Green join in as local artist Con Hunley plays the piano.

Perhaps Polian was confident that Manning possessed arguably the most important quarterback quality for an immediate transition to the NFL: brains. According to one NFL coach, Manning had the second-highest score of draft-eligible players on the NFL's Wonderlick test that gauges intelligence.

"I study the game," Manning said. "I know the game. That is my best asset."

Now more than ever, because of defensive innovations, a quarterback must be able to read defenses to succeed in the NFL. That will serve as a huge advantage for Manning, said Tennessee offensive coordinator David Cutcliffe.

"There's a lot of intelligence out there playing quarterback, but Peyton is functional because he's the fastest thinker and he has the fastest recall of any person I've been with in my life, period," said Cutcliffe. "Knowing something and being functional are two different things, particularly at quarterback."

Cutcliffe compares Manning's "instant decision making" to a fighter pilot: "It's a special quality."

But how does quick thinking contrast with escapability. In the NFC and AFC Championship games, each quarterback was mobile: Elway, Favre, Kordell Stewart and Steve Young.

"I don't think that's coincidence," said one NFL scout. "I think it's a trend. I think folks are getting so good at rushing the passer. Somewhere along the line, the quarterback has got to make them miss. With guys like Elway, Favre, Stewart, Young, Mark Brunell, Steve McNair - just because you get there doesn't mean you'll tackle them."

For that reason, some scouts liked Leaf more than Manning, who is a pocket passer. But would you rather have a cerebral quarterback or an artful dodger? One scout said its more important to be smart and have an accurate arm and quick release. He also said Manning's mobility is not a negative, it's just not a plus.

Kippy Brown is offensive coordinator for the Miami Dolphins. He was an assistant head coach at Tennessee the year before Manning became a Vol in 1994. His Tennessee contacts give him a unique insight into Manning. He thinks Manning will be an NFL star.

"You can win a Super Bowl with Peyton Manning, if you surround him with the right guys," Brown said. "I can't say that about every quarterback in this league. If you've got a chance to draft a quarterback like that, you've got to take him."

Brown thinks quarterback mobility can be overrated. Going into the last game of last season, the Dolphins, with immobile Dan Marino, were second in the NFL in least sacks allowed while having thrown more passes than any team in the league.

One coach said quarterbacks that know where to throw the football and can put it on the money, "are the guys that hurt you." It's like comparing Elway and Marino. Elway's running ability puts more

Manning signed thousands of magazines and pictures as Peyton-mania hit Knoxville from 1994-98. It's also hit Indianapolis as ticket sales and jersey sales increased after he was drafted. The Colts had one million hits on their internet sight 10 days after the draft.

pressure on the defense. Marino's quick release makes him hard to sack. Each quarterback has been to the Super Bowl. Each quarterback will be in the Hall of Fame.

Draft analyst Mike Detillier of Raceland, La., said he expected the Colts to select Manning because of his marketability.

"Peyton Manning will put more people in the seats than Ryan Leaf," Detillier said. "He's the most recognizable athlete to come out of college football since Herschel Walker. The Colts don't have a marquee player on the team."

After drafting Manning, Colts' season-ticket sales increased. Indianapolis jerseys with No. 18 - the number Manning will wear - were a hot-selling item. Ten days after Manning was drafted, the Colts' web site had one million hits. Phones in the ticket office ran nonstop the Monday after the draft, keeping seven employees busy. Numerous calls seeking ticket information came from Knoxville, Nashville and Memphis. A man in Birmingham, Ala., inquired about purchasing 400 tickets for the Colts' Sept. 6 regular-season opener against Miami.

Peyton-mania had hit Indianapolis.

"We obviously expected some feedback," said Greg Hilton, the team's director of ticket sales. "But the response has been incredible."

Even before the draft, the staff at Logo Athletic was busy taking orders for Colts jerseys bearing the name and number of their No. 1 pick. Leaf had 200 pre-orders. Manning had 2,500.

"I want to go to a team that wants me to be in that city, where the people want me there, also," Manning said before the draft. "That's very important to me. Whatever town I go to, I'd like to have the same experience I had at Tennessee. Whether that's possible, I'm really not sure."

It might be. Manning's popularity and clean-cut image - plus the fact he plays the most glamorous position in sports - should make him attractive to corporate America. Sports marketers estimate he could make over $3 million annually from endorsements, apparel contracts and appearances.

"He is everything people think he is," Polian said. "I think he'll be immensely popular here. In many ways, he reminds me of (Indiana Pacers coach) Larry Bird. He has that instinctual grasp of situations, he

Peyton Manning felt his cap and gown should have allowed him to report to Indianapolis before June 1. But the NFL rejected his appeal, even though the intent of the rule — aimed at keeping college players in school — did not apply.

has a terrific work ethic, he has an aversion to the spotlight and he's tough."

"He's almost too good to be true," said Ray Compton, the Colts' executive director of business development.

He might be good enough to immediately turn around the Colts. The New York Jets went from 1-15 to a playoff team after hiring Bill Parcells as coach. One NFL assistant said he thinks Manning can take the Colts from 3-13 to at least 8-8.

The Colts lost seven games last season by a combined 23 points. They were good enough to beat the playoff-bound Miami Dolphins 41-0. They were good enough to beat Super Bowl-bound Green Bay 41-38. Talent-wise, they probably were a 7-9 team that didn't get any breaks. They ranked 20th in the NFL in scoring and 26th in scoring defense.

Rebuilding is easier in the NFL now than it was 10 years ago, because of free agency. Several teams in recent years have shown dramatic improvement, like the New York Jets. Several have declined rapidly as well, like the Dallas Cowboys, who, in three years, went from winning the Super Bowl to 6-10.

"It's almost like it was when we were kids, choosing up sides in your backyard," Archie Manning said. "That's kind of what teams do in the offseason now, choose up sides in the backyard."

Peyton Manning's pro career should bear no resemblance to his father's pro career, in terms of team success. Despite being a two-time All-Pro quarterback, Archie's pro record was 56-130-3. Archie was sacked 337 times with the Saints. He played for a bad owner and bad coaches on bad teams.

"If I can play as long (14 years) as my father did in the NFL, plus handle things as well as he did — the media, the fans, the autographs, and do it with class — that will be a real achievement to me," Peyton said.

Notice, he didn't say anything about going 56-130-3.

Peyton starts his career by playing for a proven general manager and a proven NFL coach. Mora took the horrible Saints franchise — it never had a winning record before he arrived in the mid-1980s — and led the team to several playoff appearances. Mora also drafted two talented wide receivers to help complement Manning and talented young running back Marshall Faulk.

"If we can get Peyton some weapons, it will take the pressure off him," Mora said. "That's what we're trying to do."

Manning said he is, "really looking forward to playing" for Mora, who quit the Saints' job in disgust during the 1996 season.

Said Mora: "I got to know Peyton a little bit, not as much as people speculated I did. I know we got a quality player and an outstanding guy. We'll stick him in the mix and not sugar-feed him or go slow."

Manning was a bit frustrated that he couldn't be in the Colts' camp until June 1. An NFL rule prohibits drafted players from reporting sooner because they want collegians to stay in school. The fact that Manning had graduated a year earlier made the rationale seem ludicrous. Manning appealed to the NFL. His appeal was denied. But that didn't keep him from watching film. It didn't keep him from studying the Colts' playbook; he's had one since the day he was drafted. It didn't keep him from calling Colts coaches to quiz them about different sets and formations.

During one trip to Indianapolis, Manning met with Colts quarterbacks coach Bruce Arians, who asked Manning about some pass coverages.

"We have a pretty sophisticated offense at Tennessee," Manning said, politely.

Arians continued to ask if Manning had seen this coverage or that coverage. Manning got frustrated. Of course, he had seen those pass coverages.

"No offense, coach, but you're not talking to Freddie Kitchens," Manning said. "I've seen pass coverages before."

Manning said it didn't really matter to him if he were the No. 1 pick in the NFL draft. Don't buy it.

"Peyton wanted to be No. 1," Cooper Manning said. "It was important to him."

Manning is the third Tennessee player to be selected as the first overall pick, joining Bob Johnson (1968, Cincinnati Bengals) and George Cafego (1940, Chicago Cardinals).

"I'm proud that the Colts put their faith in me and I'm excited about what's ahead," Manning said.

Manning is the first SEC player since Auburn's Aundray Bruce in 1987 to be the No. 1 overall pick in the NFL and only the seventh since the draft's inception in 1936.

No father-son combination has been drafted higher in the NFL than the Mannings. Archie was the No. 2 overall pick in 1971, behind Jim Plunkett. Billy Cannon was the No. 1 overall pick in 1960 and his son, Billy Cannon Jr., was a late first-round pick by the Dallas Cowboys in 1984.

Peyton landed a much more lucrative contract than his father. In 1971, Archie signed a five-year deal worth $410,000. His annual salaries were $30,000, $40,000, $50,000, $60,000 then $70,000. His signing bonus was $160,000.

Manning signed by far the richest rookie contract in NFL history: almost $39 million over six years with incentives that could up the ante to $48 million. Manning got an $11.6 million signing bonus with an average base salary of about $200,000 the first three years. After the third year, the contract becomes voidable and the Colts can buy it back by paying Manning an $8.4 million bonus and giving him a new three-year deal worth over $7 million a season in base pay.

Manning's pact exceeds Leaf's. Leaf signed a five-year contract worth $25 million, with incentives that could increase the value to $31.25 million.

Before this year the highest average salary for a rookie was $3.6 million a year.

If Manning succeeds, he will buck a long-standing trend. The last SEC quarterback to start consistently in the NFL was Alabama's Richard Todd with the New York Jets in the early 1980s. Todd completed his eligibility at Alabama in 1975. The last SEC quarterback to start a Super Bowl was LSU's David Woodley with the Miami Dolphins in 1983. The SEC hasn't had an All-Pro quarterback since 1980, when Archie Manning was a Pro Bowl pick.

If Peyton succeeds, maybe Colts fans will finally stop talking about Elway. Neither Elway nor his father, Jack, were interested in John playing for then-Colts coach Frank Kush. The Elways bluffed their way out West by threatening to pursue pro baseball. And Robert Irsay, the team's late owner, wasn't willing to invest the $5 million for five years that it would have taken to sign John Elway.

"That was his right as an owner," said son Jim Irsay. "But in defense of him, you have to remember this: He had concerns about the franchise's stability. He was in Baltimore. He had that old stadium and was clearly under financial duress with the lease and declining attendance."

It's worth noting that neither Kush nor general manager Ernie Accorsi pushed the owner to sign Elway.

"Maybe if Dad had been on better financial footing and maybe if there had been a coach or a general manager or both pleading to get it done, things might have been different. The dynamics were in place to make sure Elway wasn't going to be a Colt."

So Elway became a Bronco.

And the Colts were left kicking themselves.

"There really are no 'What ifs?' in life," Jim Irsay said. "There is only 'What is.'"

What the Colts have done is clear the path for Manning to be an immediate starter. They traded incumbent quarterback Jim Harbaugh months before the draft, then later dealt backup Paul Justin, clearing the way for the team to select a quarterback.

"I believe in sticking him in there and saying, 'let's go, you're the guy,'" Mora said. "He's going to make mistakes but he's going to do a lot of good things, too."

Manning would rather be thrown into the fire than watch the flames.

"I've always thought the sooner you take your bumps and bruises, the better off you are going to be in the long run," Manning said. "But I have a lot of work to do before I'm ready to play."

Ronnie Cottrell, who recruited Manning for Florida State in 1993-94, said: "I predict in two to five years, he'll be one of the hottest players in the NFL."

When Polian was with the Carolina Panthers, he drafted Collins out of Penn State with the team's first-round pick and fifth overall. He also signed veteran quarterback Frank Reich to help Collins make the transition.

To help Manning with the Colts, Polian brought a journeyman NFL quarterback out of retirement, Bill Musgrave. Musgrave has little more pro game experience than Manning. Musgrave has only one NFL start and has played in only 11 games since being drafted in 1991 by Dallas in the fourth round.

Because of shoulder problems, Musgrave spent the 1997 season as an assistant coach with the Oakland Raiders. Indianapolis signed him the same month it drafted Manning.

In helping groom Manning, Musgrave could serve as coach, friend, confidant, roommate and/or advisor.

"I don't know how the coaches see my role," Musgrave said. "That's up to them. I'm excited to be here, get some passes airborne and help the team go in the right direction."

Manning, who shared an apartment with Musgrave for a while, said: "Bill has really been helping me out mentally. He's been in the league a number of years, and we talk about game situations and offenses. Just to have a guy like that who has been around has really helped me a lot."

Musgrave, who has made stops in San Francisco and Denver, said he's a big fan of Manning's.

"I've watched him in college at Tennessee for four years and it's fun for me to be around him, and also if he has any questions about anything in the NFL, football-wise or non-football-wise, hopefully, I'll be there as a good resource."

Musgrave is passing on knowledge he gained from playing with future Hall of Famers Steve Young, Joe Montana and John Elway.

"Defensive coordinators are so innovative," Musgrave said. "Different schemes are popping up almost every week. A quarterback has to deal with all those things flying around you, and at you."

The college book on Manning was that he got jittery under pressure. Florida players said they rattled him. Rather than take a sack, he might throw a pass up for grabs. That didn't happen often, because he holds the NCAA career record for fewest interceptions per pass attempt. But it did happen.

One Tennessee coach said Manning would have to do a better job of handling pass-rush pressure if he wanted to succeed in the NFL.

Cutcliffe, however, thinks Manning will be an excellent pro.

"I think he'll be one of the best," Cutcliffe said. "He has ability, which you have to have. And he's a fast-twitch thinker in a fast game. He is willing to work, to prepare and to be in great physical condition.

"Peyton's got plenty of arm strength. You don't need to throw it any harder than Peyton can throw it. He can stretch the field anyway you want it stretched. The only way that becomes an issue is if they make the field longer. What Peyton does best is throw the ball on time, which is what you've got to do to be successful in the NFL.

"Peyton immediately makes them a better team, and that's no slap on Jim Harbaugh, who was the No. 1 rated quarterback in the NFL in 1995. I'm supposed to believe in Peyton Manning and I do. He gave me what no other player has given me and that was complete confidence. I slept at night before games real well. I knew what to expect from him. I knew it basically was going to be done right."

A more objective observer believes Manning will be an instant success in the NFL. Vanderbilt head coach Woody Widenhofer thinks Manning will be a better pro than he was a college player. Widenhofer, architect of the famed Pittsburgh Steelers' "Steel Curtain" defense in the 1970s, devised defenses that held Manning to one touchdown pass in three seasons against the Commodores. But that's not a proper gauge to determine Manning's pro ability.

"I talked to the Indianapolis Colts for an hour and I'll tell you what I told them: Peyton Manning will be the next Dan Marino," Widenhofer said. "He has that type ability."

Polian said Manning was named the starter before training camp because he wants the rookie to get the growing pains out of the way early. "That's going to mean inefficient play at the quarterback position in the early going," Polian said.

Don't bet on it.

"Manning is advanced, very advanced," Minnesota Vikings coach Dennis Green said. "What you get in Peyton Manning is a guy who will come into the NFL and do things no quarterback has done as a rookie since Dan Marino was a rookie."

The Colts can't wait.

Manning Stats

Tennessee Career
1994 game-by-game

Game	Att.	Comp.	Yards	Interc.	TD
at UCLA	0	0	0	0	0
at Georgia	did not play				
Florida	5	3	27	0	0
at Mississippi State	23	14	256	1	2
Washington. State	14	7	79	0	0
Arkansas	18	12	157	1	2
Alabama	18	10	138	2	0
at South Carolina	23	18	189	0	3
Memphis	12	5	32	1	0
Kentucky	15	10	122	0	2
at Vanderbilt	16	10	141	1	2
TOTALS	144	89	1141	6	11
Virginia Tech	19	12	189	0	1
(Gator Bowl)					

1995 game-by-game

East Carolina	29	17	178	0	1
Georgia	38	26	349	1	2
at Florida	36	23	326	0	2
Mississippi. State	35	21	235	1	0
Oklahoma State	25	17	199	0	2
at Arkansas	46	35	384	1	4
at Alabama	29	20	301	0	3
South Carolina	20	16	215	0	4
Southern Miss	39	20	230	0	2
at Kentucky	41	23	272	1	2
Vanderbilt	42	26	265	0	0
TOTALS	380	244	2954	4	22
Ohio State	35	20	182	0	1
(Citrus Bowl)					

1996 game-by-game

UNLV	24	18	298	1	1
UCLA	28	16	288	1	2
Florida	65	37	492	4	4
at Ole Miss	22	18	242	0	1
at Georgia	41	31	371	0	2
Alabama	25	12	176	1	1
at South Carolina	36	27	362	0	2
at Memphis	40	23	296	2	1
Arkansas	41	28	282	1	3
Kentucky	23	16	317	1	3
Vanderbilt	35	17	163	1	0
TOTALS	380	243	3287	12	20
Northwestern	39	27	408	0	4
(Citrus Bowl)					

1997 game-by-game

Texas Tech	38	26	310	1	5
at UCLA	49	28	341	1	2
at Florida	51	29	353	2	3
Ole Miss	44	25	324	1	2
Georgia	40	31	343	1	4
at Alabama	37	23	304	0	3
South Carolina	25	8	126	1	0
Southern Miss	53	35	399	0	4
at Arkansas	35	20	264	1	3
at Kentucky	35	25	523	0	5
Vanderbilt	27	12	159	1	1
Auburn	43	25	373	2	4
(SEC championship game)					
TOTALS	477	287	3819	11	36
Nebraska	31	21	134	1	1
(Orange Bowl)					
CAREER TOTALS	1381	863	11,201	33	89

(Career totals do not include bowl games)

Career records: (42)
33 Tennessee
7 SEC
2 NCAA

NCAA All-time leading passers

Ty Detmer, Brigham Young	15,031
Todd Santos, San Diego State	11,425
PEYTON MANNING, Tennessee	11,201
Eric Zeier, Georgia	11,153
Alex Van Pelt, Pittsburgh	10,913

NCAA All-time touchdown passes

Ty Detmer, Brigham Young	121
Danny Wueerffel, Florida	114
David Klinger, Houston	91
PEYTON MANNING, Tennessee	89
Troy Kopp, Pacific	87

SEC Winningest Quarterbacks at each School

Peyton Manning, Tennessee (1994-97)	39-6
John Rauch, Georgia (1945-48)	36-8-1
Jay Barker, Alabama (1992-95)	35-2-1
Danny Wuerffel, Florida (1993-96)	33-5-1
Tommy Hodson, LSU (1986-89)	31-14-1
Stan White, Auburn (1990-93)	29-14-2
Bill Montgomery, Arkansas (1968-70)	28-5
Babe Parilli, Kentucky (1949-51)	28-8
Todd Ellis, South Carolina (1986-89)	24-15-3
Ray Morrison, Vanderbilt (1909-11)	23-4-1
John Bond, Mississippi State (1980-83)	23-21
Archie Manning, Ole Miss (1968-70)	21-9-1

Newman high school:

Class	Completions	Attempts	Yards	TD
Sophomore:	140	230	2142	23
Junior:	144	264	2345	30
Senior:	168	265	2703	39
TOTALS	452	761	7207	92

(includes 0-for-2 passing his freshman season)
(ran for 13 touchdowns, accounting for 105)

Eli Manning at Newman High School

Sophomore:	139	245	2340	26
Junior:	144	235	2547	24

Archie Manning at Ole Miss
1968 Season game-by-game

Game	Att.	Comp.	Yards	Interc.	TD
Memphis State	14	8	116	1	2
Kentucky	22	7	87	2	0
Alabama	26	11	129	0	1
Georgia	26	10	150	3	1
Southern Miss	39	21	255	0	1
Houston	15	6	50	2	0
LSU	40	24	345	2	2
Chattanooga	10	5	37	0	1
Tennessee	40	16	162	6	0
Mississippi State	31	19	179	1	0
TOTALS	263	127	1510	17	8

1969 Season

Memphis State	18	11	100	1	0
Kentucky	18	13	94	1	0
Alabama	52	33	436	1	2*
Georgia	28	16	195	1	2
Southern Miss	19	10	100	0	0
Houston	28	11	137	0	1
LSU	36	22	210	1	1
Chattanooga	23	12	125	1	0
Tennessee	18	9	159	1	1
Mississippi State	25	17	206	2	2
TOTALS	265	154	1762	9	9

1970 Season

Memphis State	22	17	180	0	1
Kentucky	30	12	177	0	2
Alabama	24	10	157	1	3
Georgia	31	17	254	3	3
Southern Miss	56	30	341	3	2
Vanderbilt	17	9	102	3	0
Houston	26	14	188	0	2
LSU	27	12	82	2	1
(Manning missed two games with a broken arm)					
TOTALS	233	121	1481	14	14
CAREER TOTALS	761	402	4753	40	31

*Manning set an SEC record with 540 total yards
(Manning rushed for 824 career yards and 25 touchdowns)

Author Bio

JIMMY HYAMS HAS BEEN COVERING TENNESSEE football since 1985. He covered Tennessee's recruitment of Peyton Manning and Manning's four-year career as a Vol. He has won numerous awards for his investigative reports, columns and features. In 1991, he was named the Tennessee Sports Writer of the Year. Well-versed in many sports, Hyams also has covered basketball, tennis, golf, baseball, track and field, gymnastics and figure skating. He was named the Southern Tennis Association Writer of the Year in 1997.

Hyams worked for *The Knoxville News-Sentinel* from 1985 to 1998 before accepting a job with WNOX Radio in Knoxville as co-host of SportsTalk. Hyams was a weekly guest for six years on the radio station. Hyams is the SEC football editor for *Lindy's SEC Football Annual*. He has written for *Football Digest, The Sporting News* and *Street & Smith's* basketball and football yearbooks. He also did a two-year stint as a TV guest on a roundtable sports talk show on a local station.

Hyams is a native of Natchitoches, La. He was sports editor of *Natchitoches Times* at age 16. He graduated from Northwestern State University. He also worked for the *Shreveport* (La.) *Times* and the *Baton Rouge Morning Advocate*, covering LSU Football and basketball, before joining the sports staff at the *Knoxville News-Sentinel*.

Photo Credits

7 08850 11061 9